Copyright © 2024 by Amie Turley

All rights reserved.

No portion of this book may be reproduced in any form without written permission from the publisher or author, except as permitted by U.S. copyright law.

This publication is designed to provide accurate and authoritative information in regard to the subject matter covered. It is sold with the understanding that neither the author nor the publisher is engaged in rendering legal, investment, accounting or other professional services. While the publisher and author have used their best efforts in preparing this book, they make no representations or warranties with respect to the accuracy or completeness of the contents of this book and specifically disclaim any implied warranties of merchantability or fitness for a particular purpose. No warranty may be created or extended by sales representatives or written sales materials. The advice and strategies contained herein may not be suitable for your situation. You should consult with a professional when appropriate. Neither the publisher nor the author shall be liable for any loss of profit or any other commercial damages, including but not limited to special, incidental, consequential, personal, or other damages.

Book Cover by Matt Vesper

Photography by Joely Hackmann

First edition 2024

Publishing: Starry Day Publishing

Growing Up Female

Amie Turley

©Starry Day Publishing Co.

Contents

Dedication	VII
1. Introduction	1
2. Self-Esteem	5
3. Family	41
4. Friendships	72
5. Dating	95
6. Future	139
7. Conclusion	161
Acknowledgements	163

"Here's to strong women.
May we know them.
May we be them.
May we raise them."
-Amy Rees Anderson

To the strong women I know.
The strong women who raised me.
And the strong woman I hope to inspire.

Introduction

Being a girl is hard. Like, really hard. From the moment we take our first breath, we are bombarded with expectations and examples of what we "should" be. We should be a wife, a mom, a model thin stick (but still with boobs and an ass), intelligent, helpful, happy all the time-the list can go on and on. Everyone has an opinion on what you should be and how you should act. As we get older, unfortunately, none of this changes. Every new flip of a year brings another layer of expectations and uncertainty. Quite frankly, it can be exhausting.

I have sat down to write this book hundreds of times from different angles and in catchy, Instagram-able ways. I've tried new titles and ways of mapping out the book, hoping it would grab onto my market and not let go. But that's not what we need.

We don't need another ten-step checklist to succeed or a booklet about how we find ourselves that is secretly laced with the author's own expectations. We don't need anyone else telling us who to be and how to respond to life.

So here is what we are going to do. I'm going to write about what I know and what I experienced. What I see every single day teaching teenage girls dealing with their past and gearing up for their future. No super catchy jingle to draw you in, just the raw, real truths we deal with in our lives. No censor or flashing acronyms. Just straight experience and advice. Because, yes, being a girl sucks sometimes. But it can also be sooo incredibly great. So, let's talk about things that happen and how we might handle them better. Or hey, maybe you can see how badly I tanked a situation and make yourself feel great for doing better! My knowledge and experience is yours. No filter. No censor.

I firmly believe God has a plan for every one of us. I'm pretty sure his plan for me was to do everything wrong in life so I could teach others about the lessons I learned and hopefully warn them off like a Midwest tornado siren in spring. Now, don't get me wrong, I'm not upset about my life at all. I'm incredibly grateful and have landed in a beautiful, peaceful spot. But it was a road to get here. I had so much to figure out, and unfortunately, my learning style seems to be "do it and find out." I know I am not the only one who has learned by trial and error. But you are reading about my experiences instead of someone else's because I am one of the most open people you will ever meet. I've had people in my past tell me I'd regret sharing certain experiences, but that has yet to happen. I'm so tired of feeling we can't talk and share about certain topics because it wouldn't be appropriate or ladylike. I don't care if some topics make certain people uncomfortable. When has that helped anyone?! No. You are reading my experiences because I am literally an open book (thank you for opening it). I believe we would all be a lot better off if we stripped down from the fake crap and just began being real with what we've all been through.

So, this book holds all my life lessons. The stupid things I did, the laughable heartbreak, and the ongoing trust that something greater is guiding me to where I belong. I hope you find something in this book that will help you. Maybe you'll be able to take my word on some of the mistakes and not do them yourselves. Or if you are like me and have to try it anyway, I hope it gives you a place to come back to reflect when it feels like your world is falling apart.

This book is written to be read two different ways. While I advise reading it cover to cover, you can also flip to the section you are struggling with in that moment. I reference previous chapters but always make sure you can gain understanding simply within that section. Read it through once, and then go back to the sections when you need them.

This book is for all the girls I teach every single day who I watch scratch and paw their way through life trying to find the "thing" they need. This book is for my ten-year-old daughter, who I pray daily doesn't have to experience some of the dumb things I did. It doesn't matter how much I have tried to protect her; she is still in the thick of it. But more importantly, this book is for little me. This is the book I needed growing up. These are the pieces of advice I wish someone would have preached into me. Would I have listened? Probably not. But I'd like to think so. This book is everything I needed. And since I needed it, I'm sure others do, too. This is the book every girl should read.

Self-Esteem

This is the most important chapter in this book. If you are like many of my students and only read a chapter or two before throwing the book back on your desk, PLEASE read this one. This chapter is about my favorite thing: YOU. Yes, you. I know, as I said that, you immediately got self-conscience and, if you are like me, wrapped your hands up in your oversized hoodie to "hide" away from your self-loathing and feelings. Stop it. I mean it. STOP IT. I know this chapter is challenging, but sit in it with me. Sit through the gross, uncomfortable stuff so I can tell you how amazing you truly are.

I feel like I should put a warning label on this chapter. While I have a lot to share and challenge you with, I must be upfront and honest: I still don't have this down. I still have days I wake up and mentally abuse myself all day long with insults and not-enoughness. But because of that, I have tried many things and have discovered so much about battling through this topic. And I think that is the point. Unless you are a very select few, I don't think any of us are naturally confident. We are the first to point out what is wrong with us or how we don't measure up. While I hope and pray you are of that small minority with no trauma or weird phases in life that will forever shape you, I know most of you aren't. So, let's tackle this together.

WHY AM I THE WAY I AM?

Is this not the age-old question? I spent all of my twenties simply trying to answer this. Why am I this way and how did I get this way? I'd like to believe when we are four or five, we don't have such thoughts. We can go from nap time to school to recess without being forced to confront the monstrosity that is "us." By the time I was in middle school, I could see I was weird and had issues with certain situations, but the awareness stopped there. It wasn't until I was thrown into adulthood, flooded with other adults to interact with, that I began to see we aren't all the same. We don't all handle situations or see life the same. We all have issues, but they are different. So how did we get here? Surely, we weren't born with lousy self-esteem and a tendency to overwhelm people, right?

I haven't met a person in my entire 34 years who didn't have some type of trauma or hardships growing up. I'd like to believe they are out there, but I have yet to meet one. Everyone had an experience of not fitting in or parents who, purposely or not, influenced how they see themselves. It is just a fact: We are all messed up! The first part of understanding our self-esteem is digging in and realizing why we are the way we are. Good or bad, it's important to look at your life experiences and see how they make you tick. In order to grow and evolve forward, we must understand where we came from.

School Years

The first experience most people will credit to impacting their self-image is their school life. Our friends. The lunch room. Our experiences on the playground. Your distinct feeling when group projects were presented to the class. Our school years are some of the most formative years in our development. Everything we experienced making our way through this crazy world has impacted who we are today.

For me, I was a chunky kid. Like, really chunky. I had to start wearing a bra in second grade, not because I actually had boobs but because of fat rolls acting as boobs. It did not help I towered over all the other students. By fourth grade, I was already 5'8" and looked like I could step on any other fourth grader as if I were Godzilla himself. In everyone's mind, I was BIG. Big Amie. All things big. The amount of bullying that came with being a big child is something I will never shake. Not to be dramatic, but I don't think a day went by where someone didn't refer to my "bigness." I was called a "fat brown cow" more times than I can remember. I was referred to as smelly, fat, a cow, and overall sooooo gross.

One time in fourth grade, I was at recess when a group of boys started in. Over and over again, they hurled fat insults at me. Eventually, with a broken heart, I had finally had enough. I ran straight to them with all the confidence I could muster, pushed them down, and sat on all three of them. Yep. I'm not kidding. I have no idea what I was thinking sitting on them would accomplish but I felt empowered! If they were going to call me terrible names I was going to show them just how fat I was. The best part of this story is the boys had to write apology letters to ME! I didn't get in trouble, but got my childhood bullies to write notes during the next recess.

I remember doing normal everyday activities like physical challenges, obstacle courses, or even just running that stupid mile that we were supposed to do in jeans during PE. The only thing I could think of was how I could not do it. I was too big, too out of breath, too much to help my team finish the challenge. If it required anything physical I was TOO MUCH.

Some of the worst moments actually came from something I loved: sports. Most people don't realize how something as simple as handing out uniforms can be influential to a big child. Every season, whether basketball, softball, or volleyball, the exciting day of uniforms would come. Every kid waited anxiously to see what color or sponsor they would represent that season. For a normal kid, this day was pure excitement. But as a big child, I dreaded it. You see, numbers are put on jerseys according to size in most recreation leagues. So if you were number one or two you were the smallest on the team. They went all the way up. So imagine me, in first or second grade always receiving the largest number because of my size. I never got to be a single digit like I wanted. I was always 16, 19, or even 20. This is something still happening to this day. Uniforms are essentially labeling a size on each child. Walking around as a size number 20 is something that etched my self-confidence for the rest of my life.

As you can imagine, weight has been a constant battle for me. I have gained and lost 100 pounds TWICE in my adult years. One time, in my mid-twenties, I got so tiny I was passing out while teaching, and I STILL didn't think I was small. It's pretty easy to connect the dots. Everything I went through and experienced during my school years has impacted me and my self-esteem every single day.

While this is my story, I'm sure you have a situation or experience you had during your school years that to this day, you can't shake off. Maybe it's not weight but that time you threw up in the lunch room in front of everyone. Maybe it was a week you had to wear dirty clothes to school because your family was evicted and you were living out of your car. Think back. How were your days on the playground or classroom? Were you left out for a certain reason? Did you have a childhood bully? Really take the time to think about every year of school. What stands out to you? What will you NEVER forget? Most of us don't acknowledge how much those early years affect the way we see ourselves. While I don't want you to linger on these negative thoughts, it is crucial to address them in order to understand your self-esteem. You must be able to know where you came from in order to move forward.

What We Consume

I am a 90's girl through and through. I firmly believe there is nothing better than 90's rock music and that the world was a better place when the internet wasn't made for anything more than boring business matters. I know these years were not an anomaly but like any other decade, they were a time of influence. This was the first decade to have twenty-four-hour TV with 30 or more channels. Producers had a lot of air time to entertain people. Channels were filled with bean-pole women with hip bones so sharp they could cut wood. Jeans so low you could see the model's thong and crop tops so short you could see their ribs were on every magazine page as we devoured content learning how to "Make Him Yours!".

I did not realize the impact everything I consumed had on me until I began dissecting my style way into my thirties. While looking at style after style I've come to realize all I've ever wanted are the 90's hipbones. Every pin I've pinned to try to emulate has some version of a woman with low-rise pants and a tight tank top with an inch of hips and skin showing. When I am on one of my inevitable weight loss journeys, I find I am motivated by pictures and views of what I'm aiming for. Every single picture is of pointy hipbones. I don't ever stop to admire how pretty the model is or how happy the actress appears. No, I simply am looking for hip bones ready to poke an eye out. I don't think I will ever get over the magnitude Blake Lively's hipbones in *The Sisterhood of the Traveling Pants* had on me. Sigh...

What are the hipbones in your life? What did you consume on every movie or ad until the point you longed for them? They were the picture of perfection. Boobs? A certain hair color? In the words of Sir Mix a lot, "an itty bitty waist and a round thing in your face?" Yours probably isn't pointy hips but I bet there is something you consumed over and over again to the point it has impacted the way you see yourself. Think back to the moments that defined how you see beauty. What movies or scenes stayed in your mind without asking? What magazine did you ingest at sleepovers teaching your young self how to dress and make your makeup look like? Nowadays, what pins are you obsessing over on Pinterest or accounts you are following on Instagram? I won't be the one to tell you to avoid these things at all times, though some issues justify those extremes. Instead, I just challenge you to be aware. Remember, most of the time, the "beauty" standards you are setting up in your mind are not attainable. (At least without a team of specialists and hours of photoshopping). Think back and see what has impacted you in the ways of consumption. Do you see a pattern? Are these items truthful in the way you see yourself or aspire to see yourself?

Family Impact

The final contribution to why you are the way you are is the biggest, in my opinion: our family. However you define family, it can be your greatest strength but also be your biggest downfall. Please hear me in this section, I love my family. I'm sure you love yours as well. But that doesn't erase the impact (both good and bad) they had on you in the way you see yourself. They were the very first examples you had of how society and roles were to be played out.

I have the most AMAZING women in my family. Like, we will probably have classrooms and statues dedicated to them someday, amazing. They have the largest hearts and focus entirely on others and giving service to anyone in need. Because of this extreme self-sacrificing attitude, they have made themselves "less". Now, I'm not saying the women in my family have made themselves less in a mental sense. They have been revolutionary with their thoughts, opinions, and leadership in all crowds. But as great as they are to build others up they are equally strong at tearing themselves down. I firmly believe they grew up thinking belittling themselves was a way of being humble and pure. But being humble isn't thinking less of yourself, it's thinking of yourself less.

The women in my family would do anything for other people, but if you give them a compliment, they will immediately begin to argue with you. Don't even try to tell them something about looks because they will give you not one but two reasons why what you said was wrong. My mom refused to be in pictures for years and years. If you go through the huge picture tub that every 90's family has stored away in the hall closet you will find hundreds of pictures with my mom covering her beautiful face with her hands. She was convinced she had nothing worth taking up expensive film. Growing up hearing these amazing women talk poorly about themselves obviously had a huge effect on me. I didn't realize it while I was growing up but this is why I cannot receive a compliment: I never learned how to!

One of the first moments I remember seeing this play out was one of the random times I wore something cute to church. Normally, I'd show up in jeans and some ill-fitting top, but by seventh grade, my body had changed, and once in a while, I wanted to see what would happen if I dressed it appropriately. My youth pastor gave me a compliment about looking nice and I immediately fired back with some ridiculous fake confident smirk. I will always remember when he stopped me and told me just to say thank you. I had no idea what to say or do in a situation involving praise.

Think back to how you watched the most important people in your life talk about themselves. Were they loving? Did they acknowledge the great things they did? All the same, how did they handle correction? Were they defensive and excuse-driven? Did you get taught how to love yourself and do it unapologetically?

I know the amazing women in my life were doing the best they could at that time. They were simply living out what they had been taught themselves. Generation after generation we are teaching girls the proper way to act is to tear yourself down in the name of being humble. I, for one, believe it's time to make this stop. Enough with this crap. Realize how your past affects the way you hold yourself now and try your freaking hardest to change it before passing it down again. You are BEAUTIFUL, SMART, FUNNY, ATHLETIC, LOVING, WITTY, CREATIVE, CARING, HARDWORKING. Do that unapologetically.

LIES ABOUT SELF-ESTEEM

Lie #1: Other People Make Up Your Self-Esteem

Growing up, I KNEW I had terrible self-esteem. There was no question I hated what I saw in the mirror and had the confidence of a baby deer trying to walk. What I didn't realize was who was in control of that self-esteem. As the name implies, I thought self-esteem was only dependent on me. Myself. But in reality, I was giving the control of my self-esteem to other people. I was forming my self-worth and image based on what I "thought" other people were thinking and saying about me. The problem was, no one was thinking or saying these things. Yes, as a little kid, there were bullies, but I'm talking about later on in life.

The truth was and IS that everyone is so caught up in their own insecurities and too worried about other people saying things about them that no one is actually saying anything. No one is thinking about you. No one is thinking how they can't believe you wore those earrings that make your nose look that big. Not a single person is deciding how much weight you should lose and what you need to do to somehow get a plump booty while keeping your waist tiny. No. Everyone is consumed with thoughts like that for themselves! It's a sad reality, but it is a fact. We aren't that important. Sorry to break it to you.

But this should be freeing!!! No one else has a say about you or how you feel about yourself unless you allow them. You have sole control and ownership over your self-image. So don't give that power away to anyone but yourself.

Let's pretend for a second that even one person is actually

thinking and forming suggestions about you, so what? That really just shows how miserable they are in their life. It means nothing about your self-esteem. The main point here is YOU are still in control of your self-image. You are the only person with the power to control your self-esteem. DO NOT GIVE THAT POWER AWAY!

I remember my first breakup. I mean, life devastating, thought my world was ending, breakup. I was in the eighth grade and had "dated" a boy for two years. I thought I was in love and destined to marry this boy. (So glad I didn't!) I hate to admit I was THAT girl in middle school. You know, the one making out in the corners of the hallway while everyone else is wanting to throw up? That one.

The breakup came as suddenly as the snow day that started the cold and depressing stretch of time. I was crushed. I vividly remember calling his house on repeat for hours. HOURS guys!!! And this was before cell phones so I was actually calling his home phone…disturbing his entire family. It had been a couple of weeks of heart-shattering, ulcer-growing madness before my mom finally stepped in. This was not an everyday occurrence so I knew I needed to listen to what she had to say. In between tears, she held my hands and told me I was giving control of my happiness to this boy. She urged me to take back the power. No one should have that much power. While it didn't happen automatically, it was a game-changer in the way I saw myself.

This lesson stayed with me. Whether it is happiness or self-esteem, no one can take power over you unless you allow them. It's a question I find myself surveying when I'm feeling irritable or depressed about a situation, "Who is in control of my happiness/self-esteem?" This checkpoint helps me take a step back and regulate myself. You must anchor yourself to something real and foundational. You are worthy and amazing just because you are a child of God. You didn't have to earn it or "deserve" it. It just, IS. Anchor your self-esteem and happiness to something steadfast and secure.

Lie #2: Your Self-Esteem is Permanent

Hallelujah! This one is a lie. Our self-esteem is NOT permanent! Can I get an Amen? I think we all "know" this but do we really KNOW this? When I'm standing in the mirror at a Maurice's dressing room, sampling a new pair of jeans trying not to fall into a puddle of self-loathing, do I REALLY know that I can change it? In these moments, you feel powerless-enslaved to your negative thoughts.

But if, in fact, as we discussed in Lie #1, we are the sole proprietors of our self-esteem, we are also the ones who can change it. I wish I could tell you a million ideas and secret life hacks to instantly fix your self-image, but I am not an expert in that. There are other people much smarter than I am who can help you out. Go find a book.

I can, however, tell you ideas I have tried. I am now in my thirties and actively building my self-esteem. It fluctuates more than Kansas weather. You have to baby it and check on it. The first one is to CONSISTENTLY point out the things you love about yourself. One of my favorite daily practices is writing out five things I'm grateful for in the past 24 hours. It can't be "my dog" or "my husband". It has to be more specific than that. Like, "a great walk with my dog" or "my husband making me dinner". This makes such a difference in my life viewpoint. You feel the positive and eventually begin looking for it throughout the day.

The same practice can affect your self-image. I've heard of people standing naked in front of a mirror for 5 minutes and only saying nice things about themselves. This doesn't have to be about appearance but there is something about coming face to face with yourself completely pure and raw. I've tried this before, and goodness, was it hard. The first time I think I lasted one whole minute. Eventually, though, if we point out enough things we like or affirm ourselves, our immediate feelings will begin to shift. Slowly, but surely it will evolve. Some people prefer to write these items down. If that helps you more than saying them to your mirrored image, use this as an excuse to go buy a cute journal from Target. Every single day, open it up and write five things you love about yourself within the last 24 hours. I DARE you to do this practice for a month and NOT have it affect your self-image.

Another factor that has revolutionized my self-esteem is taking note of how I see myself when I'm around different people in my life. The people you interact with daily make SUCH an impact on the way we see life and ourselves. My first marriage was a dumpster fire. I will go into more detail about that in the dating section but in short, I sold a lie of who I was. Because of this, I was never good enough for him. I wasn't nice enough, clean enough, Christian enough. I hated everything I was. I would wake up in the morning and count down the hours until I could go to bed. During this time I had the worst self-image. Every day I'd wake up and look in the mirror and not only not recognize the person staring back at me but HATED everything I saw. It didn't matter how hard I worked to accept myself, it just wouldn't work.

On the contrary, just recently, I have noticed a bit of cockiness in my life. I fully know in my heart and mind I am freaking awesome and amazing at many things! I feel like I can take on any challenge I'm faced with because I'm freaking Amie Turley! While I think a lot of things have affected this, the main one is my current husband. He has a VERY healthy self-esteem and is quick to build me up whenever he can. It has definitely rubbed off. I'm no longer finding wrong in everything but instead having to talk myself down a bit. This is 100% because the person I spend most of my time with sees the real me and loves the whole package.

The same goes for friends and co-workers. There have been many times in my life where I could tell being around someone was tearing apart my self-esteem. One of my favorite movies of the 2000s is *Mean Girls*. The main character, Kady, doesn't realize she is supposed to hate parts of herself. Up until that point, she hadn't been exposed to the regular societal experience. It isn't until her new "it" girls model what tearing yourself down looks like that she begins finding fault in her body and appearance. Yes, this is a movie, but based on very real actions. Who you are around in life makes a ginormous impact on how you see yourself.

Sometimes it's not even that deep. One of my worst adult self-esteem years was working with one of the most intelligent people I have had the privilege to collaborate with. She was my supervisor and brought so many great ideas to our program. There was never a negative or mean thing said to me but it was simply our working and production styles that set up a truly toxic environment. I needed a scoreboard. I needed to know I completed something and had done it well. She loved to keep changing things and offering new ideas. When I no longer was able to "cross" an item off my list for being completed correctly, I crumbled. I questioned every move I made and every ability I had. It took a full year to realize what was going on, and I decided I needed a change. Nothing was wrong with either person but we did not work well together. Knowing how you work and what fuels or deflates your self-esteem is crucial!

No, your self-image is not permanent. It is a living and ever-flowing entity. It has moments of peak as well as moments of valleys. But you are in control. You are the one riding in the front of the thrilling roller coaster as it goes up and down and in crazy circles. With each movement, observe and learn more about how you tick. Learn as much as you can and store it in the depths of your mind. Then keep making the best decisions and adjustments as possible. These practices, done day after day, will guide you to a healthier self-image.

TRUTHS ABOUT SELF-ESTEEM

Truth #1: You Are in Control

As we discussed during the lies, YOU are in control of your self-esteem. This doesn't mean others won't have an impact in a positive or negative way, but you are the driver. Knowing this, TAKE THE FREAKING WHEEL!!! Be in control and OWN who you are. Don't take this as a chore but an opportunity to be in control of how you and the world sees you.

I firmly believe God makes us exactly who we are at birth. In Genesis, God made Adam and Eve and said they were good. Not, okay, or in need of 30 years of experience before functional. No. They were GOOD. We are our most pure selves the moment the Lord gave us life. The problem we face is as we grow up, we adapt and change to who others tell us to be. Our parents, our siblings, society, all of these factors twist and change who we are and what we think about ourselves. Some of this is very natural and a good thing, but I believe MOST of you reading this book have spent a lifetime (no matter how long) striving to "become" something. We want to be skinnier, more loving, funnier, the list goes on and on. This tears apart our belief in ourselves. When we are constantly trying to be other versions of ourselves we never get clear and confident in who we are.

There must come a time in your life when you start the "unbecoming." You slowly tear and work away every part you have adopted that isn't really who you are, and you start releasing it. For me, this was my entire 20's. I tried so hard to be the person I thought I was supposed to be: passive, quiet, good little Christian wife. I truly gave it my all. The problem with this is it wasn't who God made me to be! So I had zero confidence in myself because I wasn't being my true authentic self! It took years of unlearning, experimenting, and working through everything I was told to be to figure out who I actually was. This is an ongoing process, but I can say I am much more confident now, knowing I am living my real, God-designed self.

Imagine waking up one morning to the siren that is your alarm clock. You drag yourself out of bed and into the bathroom. Taking a quick glance in the mirror you discover you have a face full of clown makeup on. White foundation, red nose, the works! You aren't sure when or how it happened, but BOOM, there it is. You know that isn't what you looked like, and you immediately felt repulsed by the person staring back at you. Piece by piece you start to take it off. The red nose-gone. The bright eyelids-washed away. The cheekbone spots-scrubbed. Finally, you wash the white base off the entirety of your face. Staring into the mirror you see it for the first time, yet it feels so familiar, so right. This is you. The uncovered and raw you. The perfectly made you.

What is your clown makeup? Is it your family's expectations? Clothes you think you have to wear? How to present yourself to the world? Maybe it's pressure to get married, have kids, and be a quiet little wife. Maybe it's the opposite. Maybe you are keeping up with a big-time career, knowing your true self is a stay-at-home mom. Whatever it is, you must first claim it. Call it out by name! It's insane how much more we see when we start calling situations out. Then, you MUST do the work to take each piece off. It's a long, hard process, but oh so worth it! The next time you are tempted to act like the red-nosed entertainer of your past, you must make an active choice to do the opposite. Don't allow yourself to keep dressing up in a disguise that isn't you.

When you finally get all the way down to your raw and real authentic self, your self-esteem will skyrocket. It's hard being someone you aren't. It's REALLY hard liking or loving yourself when you know you're being a fake version. Once you get down to the real you it's easy to know where and what you stand for. When there isn't any faking there is no defending, just confidence.

Truth #2: You Are More Than _____

No, the line above is not a typo. The blank is for you to fill in. Everyone has their own blank. It's that lie we keep telling ourselves over and over again that if we just had this_____ We would have confidence. If only I was skinny. If only I was smart. If only I had money. If only I was popular. If only I was an elite athlete. Whatever you find yourself dreaming about day in and day out, that's your blank. For me, it was being "skinny". I put that in quotes because there is no real definition of skinny. And even if I hit said status I still wouldn't be skinny in my mind. I swore up and down if only I was skinny, fit, and could wear whatever I wanted and look perfect, THEN everything would turn around. I'd have enough confidence to have a healthy relationship. I'd have a million friends, get the perfect job, and make millions and live happier ever after.

This is such a fairy tale and a false one at that. Because guess what, I DID get tiny and fit. I worked my tail off to lose 120 pounds in a year, but NOTHING changed. Yes, I was wearing a much smaller size of pants, but my brain and self-image were left unfazed. As we have discussed, your self-image is made up of so many things. If your blank was filled it wouldn't matter. You would find something else to hate about yourself-trust me.

Please hear me: The truth is, you are MORE than whatever you THINK you need to have in life. You are amazing and wonderful and perfectly made! You have so many things going for you! When you focus on the one thing it's laughable to the people who know you. When I hear students talk about the one thing they wished they had, I want to grab them by the face and force them to listen to me list hours worth of the gold that makes them them. It kills me to watch them focus on one tiny aspect when they are dripping with diamonds. It is where you put your focus that matters. Stop obsessing over the one thing and embrace the million amazing things you are!

THE IMPACT

Why is knowing all of these things important? Many people go about their lives without a thought about their self-esteem and what it affects. While sometimes I wish I was one of these people, I just am not. And I'm assuming since you are reading this you aren't either. We want to know why we tick the way we do and how to improve it in the direction we want to go. Your self-esteem has an astronomical impact on the way you act towards yourself and others. It has a hand in everything you do. It isn't something you can ignore and hope it gets better. You are living out your self-image each and every day.

Friendship Impact

I thank the good Lord I have friends. I can look back on my times in elementary school and junior high and I wonder how anyone talked to me. I was so insecure I would do anything for attention. Any attention was attention and I would try to get it no matter what. Learning from my older brother, I thought humor was the way to get people to like you. There are videos of me saying the craziest and most obnoxious things all in pursuit of laughter. It makes me cringe thinking about it. I thought so low of myself that I was trying anything and everything to be accepted and liked. You all know someone like this. Instead of attracting friends and people into their lives, their insecurities repulse them like poison ivy.

I see this a lot with my students in class. The ones who are mean and tear down other people are the most insecure students I have. They may not even notice it yet but it's there. They subconsciously think if they can talk bad about whomever, it will make them appear better. To be funnier, smarter, more of a catch. It is always for comparison. The worst part of this charade is not the person being insecure. It is the people they are hurting in their path.

Start looking at your friendships throughout your life. How did you come to be friends with them? Why did you stay friends? Are you still friends now? Did you act any certain way? If you really want to dissect how you acted as a friend go find a home video from when you were young. There is not enough editing software to hide the insecurities screaming from those videos.

While you cannot go back and change the way you did things it's still important to acknowledge it. I have one really good friend who I can see my insecurities influencing the relationships from the very beginning. We began playing softball together at 10. I was at the height of insecurity and annoyance to everyone around me. She and her fellow friend group excluded and left me out of so many things. I don't blame them! But in my mind she had EVERYTHING. She was pretty, funny, dressed great, had lots of friends, and I was sure could have any boy she wanted. All I wanted was to be friends with her. Because of this, I came on....hard. I tried and tried to be like her and liked by her. We didn't become friends until we were in high school and I had finally become somewhat okay with myself. No one wants a fan for a friend. A healthy friendship is two people who know who they are and just enjoy being themselves around each other. Start looking at your actions with your friends. How does your self-esteem affect these relationships?

Dating Impact

If there was ever a spot in life that highlighted my bad self-esteem, it was dating. Again, I see this every day with my students as well. I was so empty and insecure that I thought a guy or relationship would validate me. If someone would like me and want to be with me, then surely I couldn't be that bad, right? Desperation is never a productive quality in a relationship. This should be a red flag for YOU.

This inflated to much larger stakes later on in life. I dated very seriously. Like, two years in middle school, three years in high school, three years in college, and instantly married after college. I couldn't ever understand how I was having such serious relationships when all my friends were having month-long flings. I understand why now. Every guy I ever dated I wanted to be so perfect for them. I would take on their personality. Likes, dislikes, goals in life-everything. I would adapt them as my own. I had no idea I was doing this, but of course, we stayed together. Who wouldn't want to be with someone who enjoyed all the same things and had the same dreams? Although it was a great recipe for staying in a relationship, it was equally toxic. After two to three years someone would get bored and break it off. I would have a complete identity crisis because I no longer knew who I was or how to function. Eventually, I would find some other sucker and go through the process again.

This time bomb finally exploded during my first marriage. I had convinced him, genuinely thinking I was being my real self, that I was a quiet, submissive, Christian wife. I played right into the role because I felt like that was the only way to be whole or wanted. I played the role very well...until I didn't. During my unbecoming, I started to see just how opposite I was to the person I was pretending to be. I wasn't quiet. I was a loud goober who made jokes when she was uncomfortable. I wasn't a picture book Christian wife. I was a Christ follower who was passionate and outspoken and pushed boundaries sometimes. I was miserable. Any time I acted like my true self I was ostracized and put back into my place. Eventually, I just quit feeling. You can live through a lot once you have turned off all emotions. Thankfully, I'm a stubborn fighter who believes in growth and being a better person. Through this process, I finally gathered the strength to leave.

The worst part of this situation is not that I had to go through times of awfulness or that I hated my life. It was the people I hurt in the process. The person I was selling my act to had no idea what was happening. He just thought he found the perfect little wife for him. He loved me so much and would love our child as well. But he was loving someone who didn't really exist. I was like a tornado leaving destruction in my path. I tore him to pieces and our family. I'm extremely thankful for God's grace and believe we are both in loving great spots in life. But that doesn't make up for all the pain and struggle we all went through. All of this because of how insecurity affected how I dated.

School/Work/Goals in Life

I can spend a week with a new set of students and instantly point out who has a negative self-esteem. To be fair, everyone is a little insecure in their teens, but there are some who are really driven by it. Fueled by it. Restricted by it. This shows up in second-guessing their work or not having the confidence to raise their hand and volunteer. I currently teach Culinary Arts. The students who do not believe in themselves cannot, for the life of them, complete a lab without my help. Let me rephrase that. They don't need my help, they need my assurance. Is this done? How hot should it be? Does this look good enough? My first couple of months I found myself checking every group's cookies or soup to make sure it was "done". Eventually, I lectured them to have some faith in what they had learned. This happens in every area of our lives. If we do not have belief in ourselves, we cannot trust our actions and decision-making.

The biggest way I see self-esteem affect my students is when they fail. While no one LIKES to fail, only confident people are good at failing. Someone who is secure in themselves takes a failure, adjusts, and uses it to launch them forward. Someone who is insecure will meet a failure with all the drama and fanfare of a Shakespearean play. It was their fate to fail! They always fail! Why do they even try?! If we are secure and confident in ourselves it is much easier to take risks or try something new. We are able to brush it off when something doesn't work and keep going. My students who are strangled by the lack of self-confidence are the ones who refuse to try anything. They won't try a new sport, club, or skill. Recently, we were building gingerbread houses out of pop tarts, and a few kids were so terrified of messing it up that they just sat there for 90 minutes. Guys, there isn't a way to mess up a pop- tart gingerbread house. It was purely for fun! But when someone is imprisoned by their fear they cannot let themselves take chances.

This doesn't end when school years are over. Holy cow! How would my life have been different if I had believed in myself? From the first time I sat down in a padded chair and got my first brackets cemented to my teeth I knew I wanted to be an orthodontist. Every report or presentation at school was about how I would become an orthodontist. College came and I enrolled in pre-med with a track to dental school. I was THREE years into college with almost perfect grades before my lack of self-confidence started to force me to make detours. I was terrified I wouldn't get into dental school. And if I didn't get into dental school I'd have a biology degree with nothing to do with it. I didn't want to teach biology. I hated all things science unless it had to do with teeth. I quickly crumbled and ended up changing my major. While I'm super happy with where my life is now, I can't help but wonder what would have happened had I believed in myself just long enough to stick with it. There was no valid reason for me to think I couldn't get into dental school. I had top grades, tons of extra-curricular activities, and could ace an interview. But I took myself out before I could ultimately fail. This is what negative self-esteem looks like.

Every time I sit down to write this book, I have to convince myself, yet again, that I CAN do it! Confidence is a weird thing. And it always seems easier to take yourself out of a situation before you can fail at it. But this limits us so much! How will we ever grow and see what we can get better at without trying new things?

No one is great at something at the beginning. We all suck! Have enough confidence in yourself to be okay with the suck.

Every January I ask my students to set goals. I know it's corny, and students get tired of it, but I want to use that class as a lesson in believing in yourself. I share my current goals and things I'm striving for. I was sharing this a couple of years ago with a group of teachers in the room and their response genuinely surprised me. They said they were exhausted just hearing my goals. This isn't a "yeah me" moment but a UGH them! Because I know what that's like. I know what it's like to have the only goal in my year to be "get skinny," whatever that means. I know what it feels like to be so low you can't imagine yourself accomplishing anything. But if you find the courage, and consistently keep trying, I'm telling you you CAN become a dreamer. You can learn not to put limits on yourself. What's the worst thing that's going to happen? You won't accomplish them? Or not even work on them? Who cares!?!? At least you tried! It takes courage and belief in yourself just to put into words what you are aiming for. Many times, the goals change as well, and that's okay! But you moved further than you would have, had you not made some type of goal. I believe there is power in calling your shot. I think there is motivation in looking at something you want and saying I'm not afraid to go after you. Bring it. But confidence must fuel this.

SO WHAT?

If you are like my students, I know you're looking at the back of the chapter for the review. What did you REALLY need to know about this section? Here, let me help you.

Surroundings

Who you surround yourself with matters! Be around people who make you better but also love you for who you are. Find the people who allow you to be your most authentic self. I will go into more detail about this in the Friendship and Dating sections. Although no one is to solely blame for your self-esteem, you MUST be looking and analyzing how certain people affect you. This could be the most important piece to improving or maintaining your self-esteem.

Experiences

Since you get better and gain confidence the more times you fail you MUST allow yourself to have new experiences. Throw yourself into anything and everything. Find new clubs or sports to participate in. Read a new genre of book. Try a new outdoor hobby. Whatever it is, the more experiences you try the faster you will find who you really are. My 10-year-old cracks me up because I'll talk about a new food like lobster. She will immediately yell that she hates it! I then yell back, "You have never had lobster!" We don't live that life and I'm not wasting money on lobster when I KNOW she will freak out about it. Don't be like a 10-year-old. Be willing to try new things. Even if you don't like them, now you know! You've taken another step in your unbecoming.

Perfection is a Lie

Remember, perfection is not obtainable and that's okay! You are going to act like a crazy person in the middle of a party someday and walk out thinking, "What the heck?" This is part of figuring out who you are. Be okay with not being perfect. The amount of time people waste trying to be perfect is exhausting! One of my favorite people in the world spends a ridiculous amount of time trying to make everything just so. It's admirable, sure. But in the time she spends working to make tiny details perfect, other people have started a business or spent an hour dreaming and drafting goals. It's okay to make mistakes. Learn, forgive yourself, and try again.

It's a Journey

Since you know your self-image is going to change and fluctuate throughout your life, keep in mind it's a long journey. If we are lucky we will have 80 some years of changing and adapting. Be okay with being on the journey. One of my favorite writers points out to be okay with YET. You may not be comfortable in your skin YET. You may not have the job you want YET. You may not be as confident as you want to be YET. This allows you to focus on where you are going instead of what you think you are lacking.

Support Each Other

Many things make my skin crawl while teaching but the biggest ick I get is when I hear a group of girls talking about another girl. They point out they are "not that pretty" or "so crazy". I can't blame these girls too awful much because they are just emulating what they see every day. Media, adults, sports, the list is endless. Women tear other women down. We tend to be the first ones to point out a flaw in the girl on TV or the girl across the lunch room. We have GOT to stop this! We have enough people trying to tear us down we CANNOT help them. When another woman is excelling it only helps us all! Be happy for them! Remember, we are all on different paths. What is destined for them is not made for you. CHEER THEM ON! Adjust their crown, tell them their shoes are cute, and keep working towards your goals.

You are NEVER TOO MUCH

Remember in the self-esteem portion how I was always "too much" to do most anything? These words would pop up again when I interviewed for my current school. During my first semester observation, I was talking to the principal who hired me about my performance in the first couple of months. To my satisfaction, he assured me I was doing an amazing job! He would then go on to share that during my interview, he thought I was "a LOT," but he was happy with my performance. I would later find out this is the bit he shared with the department I was joining. Apparently, all of them had heard I was "a LOT". This really kicked me down for a few months. Every day I was worried about being "too much" for the people around me. I would leave a meeting wondering if I left the room thinking just how "much" I was.

You know what? F-THAT! I am NOT too much. If I was a man I'd be called a leader and offered a new role. And yes, I am a lot. I am a lot passionate. A lot loving. A lot dedicated. A lot focused. A lot of who I am MADE TO BE! And you are too! You are NEVER too much. My biggest regret up to this point in my life isn't dating in a stupid way or making an odd decision. My biggest regret is the amount of time I spent shrinking to fit into other people's worlds. NEVER make yourself less in order to fit into a box. You are made to be EVERYTHING you are. If someone else can't handle that, they can move along.

CONCLUSION

The last thing I want to say to you about loving yourself I wish I could be sitting right in front of you to say. I would look you right in your eyes and remind you that you are freaking...amazing! You have so many wonderful things that make up you it BLOWS MY MIND! Every day, I see my students, and I WISH they could see themselves from my eyes for just a second. Maybe then, they'd see just how amazing and gifted they are. That they are made to do unbelievable things! That they are worth any and everything in this life. They are absolutely perfect the way they already are. Love yourself as much as I- and the people around you do!

Family

Family. What a loaded word, right? Family means something different to everyone. I actually think family is the most complicated topic in this book. I'm not going to sit here and assume everyone had the same family experience as I did because I know that's not true. I fully understand some of you have been raised by one parent, or your grandparents. Maybe you have been in foster care your whole life, and as heartbreaking as it is, you don't really know what a family is. I fully recognize for many of these situations, I am not suited to give advice. I can only write what I know and hope even a small piece of it will help you.

What I have found while reflecting and being a part of numerous families over the course of my life is that there are pretty consistent family roles. This doesn't mean every person in your family must play a certain role but certain roles exist and are needed in order for a family to function. Any parent can play any role or a mixture of roles. The same goes for siblings or even with your own role. We all play naturally into our spots and they can change over time. I have changed my parenting role many times over the short ten years of my daughter's life. This is the same for your family-however that may look.

Let me also preface this section by saying that if you don't have someone in one of these roles, that is OKAY! Don't we all wish we came from a perfect *Leave it to Beaver* world? I know I just aged myself with that reference but let me tell you. Even the families that appear perfect have their own mess of struggles. So don't worry if you think you are missing one of these people. We all are filling in where we can.

CAREGIVER/MOM

The first role we are going to look at is the caregiver. For many, this is mom. Others this may be a grandparent or father. This is whoever gives you the emotional support and care throughout your family. This person empathizes with you and is the one you run to when you've achieved a goal but also when you've fallen down and skinned your knee. You are emotionally connected with this person.

For me, this was my mom. She was a very traditional 80's mom. She made sure the house wasn't falling apart, food was on the table, and that my brother and I knew how to act in public. She was very kind and loving. She was my biggest cheerleader in whatever I did! She would immediately tell me "Great job!" after a softball game even though I walked ten people. It didn't matter. She was and still is, my biggest fan.

If you didn't grow up with someone in this role you may find it hard to open up and be emotional with people. One of my favorite student's mom left her family when she was very young. She doesn't have many memories of her at all. While we talk about lots of things, many of our conversations are about her relationships and how everything gives her the "ick". You know, the feeling like your skin is peeling off and you are about to throw up? She has found it incredibly hard to show real love and emotion towards her friends and now, boyfriend. She agrees; it's because even though her dad was awesome, she never had the emotional and compassionate figure in her life to teach her about feelings. Maybe this is you too. Can you pinpoint the person in your life who was always emotionally there to help and guide you? How has having or the lack of having this person impacted the way you handle emotions today?

Insights

So many of my insights for this role come from being a mom myself. There were so many things I thought I knew or thought I understood but had no idea until I was a mom myself. The number of times I have texted my mom and apologized for not trusting her is incalculable.

The first piece of insight is your caregiver/mom isn't perfect. I can remember being a kid and thinking my mom had everything together. She knew all the answers and could do anything in this world. I had my daughter the same age as my mom was when she had me and HOLY COW! There is no way she had everything together in her 20s. She had me when she was 24 and my brother when she was 21. No 21-year-old out there has their life together yet. I think the best thing you can realize about your caregiver/mom is they are still working on their "stuff". They are going to mess up. Every single night, they will lay their heads down, wondering how they even made it through the day and how they will survive tomorrow. They are still carrying their own baggage from when they were your age. Even if they are working hard to sort it out, it is still going to affect how they show up for you.

Remember this when you're mad at one of their decisions or after they blow up on you for what seems like no reason. They are going to be imperfect. Give them some grace. See past the times they mess up and focus on the times they are great.

One of the times I really let my imperfection show while parenting was when Charleigh was three. She loved Disney princesses and wanted to dress up like them every day. The day after Halloween, I went to Walmart and bought every single princess costume all at 75% off. This was going to be a huge part of my sweet girl's Christmas. This also meant I had over a month to hide them and keep her from getting into them. If you've ever been around a toddler, you know this is almost impossible.

One day, I was working in my office while she was in there playing. This was a normal thing for us so I could watch her while being productive. Focusing in on my current tasks, I let her roam for just a second too long. She had pulled a bag out of the closet and found a turquoise and pink Ariel outfit. Her eyes lit up for a brief second before I lost it. In utter surprise and "Oh crapness," I yelled, "What are you doing?!" in the worst tone possible. Rightfully so, she fled off to her room in tears, not understanding what she did to get yelled at so hatefully.

I immediately felt like the worst mom in the world. I'm sure this is one of many examples of my own inability to process my emotions fast enough to respond outwardly, which hurt her. Needless to say, I apologized and tried to explain myself to the weeping sweetie. She also got her costume a month and a half early. Allow your mom to be imperfect because there is really no other option.

The second insight is all about mom/caregiver guilt. This person in your life cares so deeply for you they will second guess everything they do. Let me tell ya, that mom guilt is REAL. That last insight about your mom not being perfect? No one knows that more than HER! Every night she goes to bed tearing herself apart about what she could have done better or what she didn't do for you. Trust me. Every time she yells at you or forgets to bring you the correct pants for your game she beats herself up over and over again. This is not only from the pressure society has put on her but just the pressure and expectations she has put on herself. She loves you so much and wants to be absolutely perfect for you. Realize this in how you are interacting with her. Reassure her when things are great and tell her you forgive her when she messes up. The single fear each parent has is screwing you up irreversibly.

Finally, the thing to know about the person in this role is they genuinely want to trust you and let you experience things. They want to allow you to go to that party or try that new club. They want to let you go and to have fewer rules and restrictions. But this is not always feasible. Because of their own fears or maybe your actions, they have put on multiple layers to protect you. No, you can't drive at night because Sally down the street crashed into a pole right as the sun went down, and now your mom can't stop picturing it happening to you. She doesn't want to have to check in with parents that you are where you say you are but remember that time you were actually at the park instead of at Sarah's house? This moment hasn't stopped scaring her. Every time she wants to let you prove yourself again, her fears come crashing back. Are they real? Are they warranted? Probably not. But it's reality. If you remember this, you will see your mom/caregiver in a whole new way.

Because of this truth, I must URGE you not to break your caregiver's trust. Nothing makes us more freaked out than when you start lying about what you're doing. It is so hard to earn trust back…with anyone…but especially someone worried about your safety. I've had conversations with students who have blown it big. They've lied about where they were and have no idea what to do next. I always tell them the first step is to admit you were wrong. Your parents want to give you trust and freedom, but you must prove that you are mature enough to handle it. This means owning up to your mistakes. While admitting you were wrong may not restore trust instantly, it will help open up the lines for healing to begin.

Actions

The number of diverse conflicts you can have with your mom is absolutely endless. There is not enough space in this book to discuss every one and how to handle it, but we are going to talk about the most common ones.

Tone of Voice

The first one is tone. Remember all the times she has said it's the tone of your voice? It REALLY is. Don't argue with her. The way you speak can sometimes sound so hateful and disrespectful. This is an instant recipe for your mom to get frustrated. Trust me, I know, so many times we are already frustrated because of something else so the tone just immediately jumps out. But when this happens, the worst thing you can do is deny it. Really. I mean, have you ever heard someone tell your mom she was wrong? How did that go? In the heat of the moment and screech of the tone, just admit it.

I still do this to my mom today and I'm 35. I also do it to my husband. I'm having a conversation in my head about the mountain of laundry I still need to do when he asks where I want to eat. My hateful tone responds with I DON'T CARE! Instantly, I have heard myself and feel awful. Here's how to handle this. IMMEDIATELY, acknowledge that what you said came out with a tone and apologize for it. The moment you take responsibility for your actions you are showing your caregiver that you are maturing and realizing you aren't perfect. This is a HUGE moment in the daughter/mom relationship. Will you still get in trouble? Maybe. But that's not the point. The point is taking steps to acknowledge where you fail and how you are reflective enough to do better.

You Do Not Know Everything

Along these lines, remember you DO NOT know everything. Oh goodness, I knew everything. I was a wonderful student, president of everything, and I knew MY reality. I thought my mom had no idea. She had no advice to give or a bigger picture to share with me. This is the single biggest thing I got wrong growing up. I'm not sure what is in ourselves when we are young that we want to prove we know things. We know what's best for our lives! I think it's part of our internal need to prove ourselves. Stop. Just stop. You aren't supposed to know it all yet so don't try to pretend. Your mom brings a wealth of knowledge and experience to your life. Believe it or not, she used to be pretty cool! She had her own life and dreams. Listen to her. She may not be right about everything but she is worth listening to. You can learn so much if you open up to her advice and direction.

While you are listening and learning from her, be honest. I mean TRULY honest. The first time I was forced to be 100% honest with my mom was when I was telling her I had gotten pregnant. Yeah, not the best time to try something new. And for me, I had no reason not to be honest with my mom. Yes, I'm sure she would have disliked many things I was doing or had done but if I could, I would go back and go through the uncomfortable in order to gain real advice from her. I encourage you to be honest. Be open. She already knows more than you think, anyway. You might as well keep the lines of communication open. This will only improve your relationship with her and the outcomes of your life.

Empathize

Empathize with your mom/caregiver. Remember all those insights I just gave you? Keep those in mind. When it's a day before Christmas, and your mom is running around the house trying to make everything perfect, remember she is doing that for you. It's not her fault her mom passed down the need to prove herself through entertaining. Be aware she's just going crazy because her mom is on the way and will make a comment about every single thing. Take the time to observe and truly try to understand why your mom is the way she is. I have found I am a lot more forgiving when I empathize and think about the WHY behind my mom's actions.

I had a moment only about a year ago that brought me to real tears. I am not a very emotional person (more on that in future chapters) and I'm not very raw or real with my mom. We say I love you freely but we are of the lower middle class where the women suck it up and make it work. We are still working on being real and raw. One of the things that has always driven me nuts about my mom is the fact she will NOT choose specific plans. For instance, she won't choose where to eat. She won't choose what time we are leaving to go shopping. She won't choose what SHE will make for dinner that night. Because of this, it tends to fall on me. Over and over again, I am making these decisions for the entire group, and then I'm worried about whether they were the right choices or not.

While digging through my own crap, it suddenly hit me. My mom had survived growing up and in her marriage by doing the least resistant option. If she allowed her dad or my dad to choose then it couldn't come back on her. This is how she kept the peace in a toxic world. When I came to this understanding, it BROKE me. I mean, I sobbed driving down Interstate 435. All of a sudden, I had empathized with my mother deeply enough I understood. I saw just how hard it was for her to make these decisions. I called her and, in between tears, apologized for being so mad about it. I told her I finally understood. And because I understood, I don't mind making the decisions now. I gladly do this to take the heat and anxiety off of my mom.

MOST parents out there are truly doing the best they can at that moment. They are giving it everything they have, and in that moment, it may be a little erratic and crazy. But if you empathize with your mom during the hard and the great times, you will grow an understanding and admiration like never before.

Appreciation

Finally, appreciate your mother/caregiver. I mean it. Appreciate the hard work and time she puts into everything for you. Appreciate the nights she stays up awake worrying about how she screwed you up. Appreciate the meticulous planning she does getting ready for a holiday. Appreciate the growth she has made while dealing with her own crap all in the name of being a better mom for you. Appreciate she is there for you every day and is truly doing the best she can in that moment. Appreciate her and TELL her you appreciate her.

One of the greatest notes I have ever received was from my sweet girl this past year. I had been finishing up my second master's and feeling terrible for it taking time away from her. While I was in bed thinking about just how hugely I had failed that day, she came into my bedroom with a huge cup of ice water and a note saying, "Love you, Mummy." And no, we aren't English, this is just how cute and real it was. It was perfect! It was everything at that moment I needed. You can still find that note tapped to my bedside table. It is a constant reminder that despite the complaining and demanding, my sweet girl appreciated me in that moment. She empathized with what was going on and went out of her way to let me know I was loved. Those little moments are everything to your mom/caregiver.

RULE ENFORCER / DAD

This role is the person who forces rules and expectations on you but not with the same emotion as the caregiver role. They step in when needed and bring the hammer down. This may be your dad or grandpa. This role gets a little murky for me. For lots of reasons that will wait until another book, my father was not my father growing up. My mother had to be in this role for most of my life, too. It was like she switched. I know she wasn't the only one.

When I was 10 years old, I was asked to join a competitive softball team whose coaches would change my life. My coaches would quickly become my father figures. From putting up with me as an insecure 10-year-old to walking with me on softball senior night, both of them were always there and filling this role for me. Who is it for you? Who was the person in your life who supported you but also brought rules and expectations to your life? Was it a grandpa, mother, father, or someone who stepped up?

If you didn't have someone in this role, you may see some impact on your life. The amount of "daddy issues" I've had to deal with could take up a book on its own. Maybe you are constantly trying to fill a void for protection. This shows up with a long line of guys you've dated. Over and over again you have tried to find someone who would protect and keep you safe. My friends like to joke about my attraction to older men. My first husband was 10 years older than me and my husband now is 15 years older. Coincidence? I think not.

Insights

Many of the insights for this role will be similar to the caregiver role as they really work best together. The first is to give them grace because they aren't perfect. While I've never been in this role myself, I have watched my "Dads" work through it and try to be better. Dads are just like moms. They aren't perfect. They are trying their best and want to be great for you but they are dealing with their own crap. They are unbecoming what they were taught to be and are trying to be everything a new generation needs. I'm sure it's exhausting. Every time they holler like their father did to them I'm sure they sit and tear themselves up. They promised to be better but they've found themselves smack dab in the middle of the same life. Be forgiving and understanding.

Since most people in this role tend to be men, let's take a second and look at how men have been raised the past couple of generations. My grandfathers were raised to provide for the family and be the "man". They weren't allowed to have emotions or dreams or feelings. I cannot imagine how trapped they must have felt. What a miserable life! Work all day at a laborious job, go home and sit in a chair, and do it all over again the next day?

While generations since then have started to make a switch, you can still see the impact. The struggle is there. They want to provide and be everything they were taught to be, but they also want to share their feelings. They want to open up to their kids and show their love but for some, it's still very hard to do. The balance of who they were taught to be and who society is telling them to be is a chasm the size of the Grand Canyon. My husband is one of the greatest dads in the world and he still struggles with being everything his children need.

I think a common theme many father figures have is the feeling that it is up to them to keep everything afloat. They must make sure the bills are paid, the family is fed, and their kids know how to act. (Remember these from the mom section too?) In our world today, it takes everyone to survive in a family but a father figure is still going to carry the weight on themselves. And what's worse, many do not feel allowed to talk about it or show weakness. This is still something they are working on. I hope and pray this gets easier with every generation. Can you imagine feeling like you are holding every person on your back and NOT being able to talk or vent about it? While it's not your issue that he feels that way, it is your job to acknowledge when this is happening, empathize with your father, and extend grace when you can.

A big insight I've discovered about the father figure is everything they do is fueled by their need to keep you safe and respected. They take this as their main role. So when they don't allow you to drive across the country by yourself, there's a reason. They aren't trying to be killjoys or jerks; they are desperate to keep you safe. If anything happened to you, they would take full accountability for the actions because it was their role to keep you safe. Of course, control is all a big lie, but they are still going to try!

For the life of me I could not understand why my dad always seemed so angry when we went on trips. Worlds of Fun or a simple drive through downtown Kansas City would leave my dad yelling for no reason that I could see. I could not understand why I was getting yelled at in scary situations when I wasn't doing anything wrong. (Although I'm sure running my mouth didn't help the cause). After a heated afternoon, my mom let me in on the secret: men tend to sound angry when they are scared. When a father figure gets frightened, they come across as angry. They are short, rude, and may even yell at you. Again, this is not warranted but understanding this will help you see through the anger. More often than not, when the safety sets back in, they will apologize and return to their normal selves.

The other situation that fuels their actions is their need for you to be respected. As I've mentioned, I have NO idea what goes on through a man's head. I have learned a lot from being married twice and having a brother but their crazy minds puzzle me to this day. This showed up many times when my older brother would take on the role of a father for me. Four years older, he went off to college while I was entering high school. This was 2003 and cellphones were a very new thing. Very few kids had them and parents were just starting to carry them.

After he came home from college for the first time he pulled my mom aside and lectured about how crucial it was for me to have a phone. While I have no idea what he saw or experienced those first few weeks of college it was enough for him to feel the need to protect me. A couple of months later, I was one of the first freshmen in my school to carry a cell phone.

This came from a truly protective mindset. My brother didn't care that I had the means to play Snake any time I wanted or send 100 texts each month. He wanted to make sure wherever I was and whatever situation I was in, I was able to reach someone. I truly think this was one of the greatest acts of love he ever did for me as a father figure.

Protecting a daughter's respect isn't more prevalent than during sports. I've seen some crazy softball dads in my lifetime. And while I don't always agree with their actions their motives are always pure. They want their daughters respected and their hard work to be respected. When they see someone not respecting them they will lose their minds! I've seen yelling, cursing, and overall embarrassing behavior. Watching this as a coach makes me frustrated and want to say something. But I remind myself, though it's not warranted, it comes from a good and loving place.

One of the funniest moments of my adolescent dating era was when a guy I had dated for a few months went off and cheated on me. This obviously made me feel like trash and less than dirt. Well, my brother and adopted brothers were still in high school at this time and on the same wrestling squad. I have no idea what was said that weekend, but I do know he never bothered me again. While this may not have been the best way to handle the situation it was solely driven by respect. When your father figure yells at you for wearing an outfit they don't approve of, it really isn't them trying to be a jerk. They simply want everyone to respect you as much as they should. Take a breath, listen, and take it for what it is.

Actions

Grace

While I can't give a load of advice here, I can give some suggestions. The first is the same as with the caregiver role, empathize and give grace when needed. Try to see their struggles and try to understand why they are the way they are. Even more, be open enough to ask them! I find while it's often uncomfortable, the father figures in my life have been some of the most honest and wise people around me. I simply needed to start the conversation. I had to take the first initiative and ask for advice or ask why they reacted a certain way. They will normally give it to you straight, whether it hurts your feelings or not.

Where's The Love?

I think every girl, at some point, finds it challenging to see the love from their father figure. They think he doesn't care and doesn't give them attention or time. I felt the same way growing up with my father. As I've gotten older and have experienced more of these situations, I can see now it's not normally the truth. It's simply that the way they show their love isn't the same as you. While you may want direct words to know they love and care about you they may not ever give you that. Instead of an "I love you" before you leave, it's a "Be safe, don't wreck the car." Instead of hugs and affection they light up and smile any time they are proud of the things you are doing. While I believe there is power in sharing your desire for certain love and affection, it is also a good practice to see and understand someone else's ways of showing that they care and appreciate you.

Listen

This last action step is hard for me to type out because of my own pride-but listen to your father figure. For whatever reason, I hated taking advice from father figures more than anyone else. I assume that's because most of the time they were right. It would drive me crazy to get advice from someone I thought had no idea what I was going through. While that may have been true at times, they are giving a DIFFERENT viewpoint on the situation, and that is one of the most valuable pieces of advice you can receive. They look and experience life in an entirely different way. Listen to what they have to say and truly take it to heart.

As I mentioned, my brother and softball coaches gave me some amazing advice during my formative years, and I ignored just about all of it. But now, as a 35-year-old woman who has gone through allllll the things, I can tell you, if I had listened and taken their advice, I could have saved a lot of time and heartache. Drop your pride, and listen. Who's advice would you want more than someone whose main role is to protect and respect you?

SIBLINGS

Chances are you are one of the 80% of people in this world who have at least one sibling. Whether older or younger, you had someone who was there all the time trying to share everything. I grew up with a brother four years older than me. Without trying, he influenced me in ways I will never fully understand. He was the example of what I should be and who I WANTED to be. No one was cooler than my brother. While most of the time I was a fan, we also had plenty of moments when I wished he hadn't been born. As he was literally body-slamming me off the couch after watching an hour of WCW, I mentally begged to be an only child. Siblings are hard. It doesn't matter the age or gender; any time you are living that closely together and trying to grow and develop, many challenges are going to arise. Remember, your siblings are going through the same challenges and growth as you are!

Again, if you don't have any siblings or have siblings so many years apart you basically grew up an only child, you may still have this influence. My amazing grandmother was an only child. But she was NOT without siblings. One of my favorite people in the world ended up being like a sister to her. I grew up knowing these ladies as my grandma's sisters not extended family. Look around you. Who plays that role for you?

Insights

The first insight to remember about any type of sibling you have is you are all fighting for the same things. Underneath, everyone wants to be seen, loved, and taken care of. Since there is a limited supply of love and attention to give from the people in your life you are already set up to be in opposition. It doesn't matter how well you get along with your siblings; there are times you are going to be at a head. Remembering at the end of the day you all want the same things and need to share the time, affection, and supplies will help you see your siblings' actions for what they are. Maybe they need more attention from Dad. Maybe they are mad for feeling like their rules are different than yours. Kids are all different. And how parents and caregivers parent each child must be specific to that kid.

My best friend in the entire world was raised in a family of four kids. She was the youngest. I remember repeatedly the times her older siblings complained that she got to do things they didn't at her age. Or vice versa-curfews for her were much stricter than her siblings. The fact is, we grow as parents and adapt to the specific kid.

I personally, didn't need as many strict regulations because I was in a constant state of trying to please. It didn't matter if my parents gave me a strict curfew or wouldn't let me talk to a certain person because I was already a step ahead of them and overcompensating trying to be good enough and perfect. This is completely different than my brother. He needed to test every boundary my parents put forward. I'm sure you can see how this would set up some resentment towards each other. While I just thought my brother was a mean brute, I'm sure many times he thought I got away with an easy set of standards. Because of these types of situations, it is crucial to remember both of you want to be loved and supported and to grow up as quickly as you can. Empathize with your siblings and try to see the situations through their eyes.

Another important insight with your sibling roles is the fact they are going to change throughout your entire life. The way my brother and I interacted when we were young is 100% different than the way we interact now. I've heard many people share how their relationships with siblings got so much better when the first one moved out and onto the next phase in life. When siblings are no longer living in the same quarters fighting for the the same things they can begin to appreciate each other for who they are.

Be ready for the changes and adapt as you can. But my biggest insight and plea is to love your siblings no matter what. No one else in this world is as similar to you as a sibling. You have come from the same place and share so many important experiences together. Do your best to understand them and make lifelong friends with them. It can truly become a beautiful thing.

Actions

Empathize

Like all the other roles before this, the number one action step is empathizing with them. Try to put yourself in their shoes and understand what they are going through at the time and why they act the way they do. This is never an excuse for poor behavior, but if you take the time to really relate and understand where your siblings are coming from, what you discover will blow your mind.

My dad LOVED to talk about my brother. I think he was everything my dad wished he would have been. As a very young, insecure, child I did not take this well. I wanted to be bragged about and seen just as much as he was. I wanted more than anything, for my dad to talk about me. Brag about me! Later on in life, I would finally see by brother's point of view. He had his own mess of issues from always being talked about. He had a lot to live up to and it wasn't always easy. There was an ENTIRE other side to my reality. Looking at situations with your siblings from THEIR point of view can help you understand their own struggles and hardships.

Stand Up For Yourself

A controversial action step is to stand up for yourself! I will always be the first person to ask you to look at a situation from someone else's point of view but sometimes you just have to stand up for yourself as well. Make sure you aren't taken advantage of in a sibling relationship. If you aren't receiving the care and treatment you need, say something! I tried this many times in my life and was beaten into sibling submission. But I still think you need to voice your needs or boundaries.

Follow and Lead

Finally, with any sibling dynamic, it is important to be able to follow AND lead. There are many times in this life you need to be a good follower. Learn from someone else and take everything in you can. Also, know when you are the one someone is looking up to. If you are an older sibling I guarantee the younger one in your family is looking up to you for how to act and what to strive for. Do not take this responsibility lightly. This doesn't mean you can't fail because, again, we aren't perfect. But with every action and decision, know someone is watching and modeling their lives after you. Because whether you like it or not, it's happening. Give them something positive to look up to.

SO WHAT?

There are two points I really want to drive home for you. These are valid for any of the roles we have talked about previously, but also for any extended family I didn't talk about. Your grandparents, cousins, aunts and uncles. Whoever this is for you, they are just as important! My daughter has lots of bonus aunts with my four best friends. These people are just as important and sometimes even more involved as real blood relatives. Whether it's your mother figure or a second cousin, these last two points are important for them all.

The first one is to MAKE TIME for them. I can tell you that as you get older, it is a fight to stay connected to your friends. Some will stay and some will go off on their own lives. But your family, is connected to you forever. The wealth of knowledge and experience that all of these people in your family possess is a living and breathing Google for you to tap into. Take the time to stay connected to your family. Ask about their life. Be excited for what makes them excited. Show them you care! Make sure to come to your family's summer party. Make the time to keep these people in your life.

When you do have these moments with them, be PRESENT. You can call me an old fogy if you want, but if you are going to your grandmother's house for Thanksgiving and have an Air Pod in the entire time, you might as well not be there. You are missing out on some of the richest experiences you could have. Be THERE! Ask them questions about their life, about how they grew up, or what they do now. Document these things deep in your mind. I'm telling you, someday you will be so thankful you did. While I grew up with many of the same distractions you have today I am SO thankful I took the time to be close to my grandparents. They are some of the most amazing people in this world and I am lucky to know them. I guarantee there are these same jewels in your family whether they are blood or not. But you have to put in the time to build the relationships and stay connected to gain their wisdom and knowledge.

Recently, I have been able to get closer to one of my aunts. She is more like me than my mother is. To really get to spend time with her is like watching where I come from acting out in front of my eyes. Many times, I wasn't sure how I ended up the way I am, but by getting to know that extended piece of my family, I can see I am genuinely still a part of this lineage. She has the most amazing mind and spirit. She has tackled some of the hardest things in this life and has still found a way to persevere and rise above. I want to emulate her in so many things. If you put her and my mother together it's like the absolute greatest of both worlds. THIS is why you want to connect to family. It gives you a much more complete view of your family and where you come from.

The second important point about family is to not be afraid to establish boundaries. Goodness, this one is hard. I wish I could say I am a model of this concept, but I have just started to set boundaries in the past year or two. Part of that is building up my self-esteem and knowing who I am and why. Once you do this you may begin to see and feel when you are not at peace. This goes for all family. I will never say to easily and swiftly write someone off from your life but I DO believe there are times you need to. My father hasn't spoken to his siblings in at least 20 years. He had to create a boundary in a very toxic situation for him to get better. My husband has done the same thing with one of his sisters. After years and years of trying and putting up boundaries, there was a time when it was just too much. The toxicity was all that was left.

Not every situation is this deep. A boundary I recently tried to put up is with my own father. Since neither of us knows how to handle emotions within a father/daughter relationship, we have always had very odd interactions. This past summer, I put a boundary up asking for one of his actions to stop, and it was not handled very well. Although I wish that wasn't the case it was only the first time a boundary was extended. I now feel more comfortable putting those boundaries up and enforcing them. It is so important to know that you are worth being treated a certain way and wish to feel a certain amount of peace. While your family doesn't have to understand that, they should definitely respect it. Give it time, be consistent in your stances, and be aware of when it is time to step away.

CONCLUSION

While this chapter had a lot of advice and random ideas shared with you I really hope you pull out one major thing-empathy. This life is not easy. Being your father figure is tough. Being a mom is exhausting. But if we all start taking a step back and try to understand where that person is coming from and why they think the way they do, you will be amazed at how much more you understand and appreciate each other. This is not the same as making excuses for someone, but trying to bridge that gap between excuse and understanding.

Take the time to look at their entire picture and don't be afraid to ask them questions. When the timing's right (not when you are already 20 minutes late for work and school) take the time to ask your family why they think or do certain things. Most of the time they will be willing to share with you. Or maybe they don't know themselves! It takes another person to point out certain attributes to us before we can be aware of them ourselves. Allow yourself to be present and committed to whoever makes up your family and try your hardest to understand them. Isn't that what you want back from them? Empathy and understanding? Can you imagine a family dynamic in which we all sought to understand and learn from each other?

Friendships

One of the parts of life I get asked about more than anything is friendship. Having friends is an essential part of our lives but goodness is it hard. Not only are you trying to grow up and figure out your crap but now you are trying to do it while having the company of someone else equally messed up. Friendships can be the greatest and most beautiful part of growing up female but with some sound advice.

I think even 10 years ago I may have omitted this part of the book. I had some really great friends and didn't seem to have too much advice to give. But as I've gotten older I've found that to be completely untrue. I just had to get far enough away from the normal friendships to see how special, yet complicated friendships can be. So keep this in mind. If you are right in the middle of your teenage years or even the beginning of your twenties you may not be able to "see" a lot of these ideas or situations. I promise you, they are there.

A huge misconception we all fall into with friendships is grouping them together all under one umbrella. A person is either a friend or not. They are either a yes or no. It's computer binary code 0 or 1. There are no other options. But friendship is not that exclusive. There are as many unique types of friendships as there are people on this gigantic planet we live on. Some are here for a season while others are your BFF's for life! Some you only see while at work or school, whereas others are the people who will help you get through the hardest parts of your life.

All of these friends are valid and IMPORTANT! What we tend to do though, is lump them all together in expectation and treatment. We need to begin looking at friends for what type of friends they are and value them for that and that alone.

TYPES OF FRIENDS

Acquaintance Friend

The first type of friend is one I like to call an acquaintance friend. This is the person you follow and casually like their new picture of their dog on your mini feed. You make sure to post a birthday

GIF on their special day only because Facebook reminds you. You don't have their phone number to text or call to tell them and wouldn't even if you did. You are friends with these people but just slightly. You would help them if they asked but you don't go out of your way to check on them or spend time together. Many times these are friends of friends or people you have met once.

These friends are so lovely to have! I like to think of them as the extra blanket you take to a bonfire. They don't do the full heating of your body like your coat and sweatpants but it is just the extra you need to make your comfort whole. These friends are wonderful to have and fill up the extra parts of your life. When you are scrolling through Facebook or Instagram while waiting at the doctor, these are the beautiful people you catch up on. Acquaintance friends bring you smiles and inspiration from afar.

My favorite thing to catch up on with my acquaintance friends is their beautiful families! I receive just a smidgen of joy when they post a picture of their new baby or announce a new promotion. These friends are so great to have around in your virtual world as LONG as they are positive.

I had to break up with one of my acquaintance friends recently. I know that sounds dramatic but it really is a thing. I don't think I have ever spoken to this person, and if I have, it was once in elementary school. I enjoyed watching this person from afar but recently found myself down one too many rabbit holes late at night when I should have been sleeping. Once realizing he was on his fourth fiancee of the year I decided it was time to move on. This was truly not in a judging way, but if an acquaintance friend begins adding drama and anything but extra JOY to your life it's time to remove them. The best part about the removal process is that it's swift and clean. I simply unfollowed them. Simple as that. No emotion, they didn't even know, but the friendship was over.

It's important to look at who is this type of friend and acknowledge them for what they are. Appreciate the joy they bring but don't be upset when you don't get invited to their wedding. Admire, receive joy, and make sure to give joy back. These acquaintance friends may just be what you need when you need a little extra layer late one lonely night.

Situational/Proximity Friends

My sweet girl had a ROUGH year in 4th grade. When I say rough, I mean ROUGH. I wasn't sure we were going to make it through. The level of drama and issues were so vast at times I thought about dropping wine off at her teacher's house. All year I prayed and worked to figure out how to fix the constant issues a group of them were having. After a great summer, it was time for 5th grade. While I had my concerns, it is astounding how GREAT of a year she is having. She has close friends, doesn't get in trouble, and hasn't been to the counselor near as much! This is all because of who her situational friends are. I'm sure you can remember being in elementary school and feeling like your world revolved SOLELY around the 20-25 people who were in your class. They were your only options. Most of the day, you had to survive, finding solace within that small group of people. This is how situational friends work.

Situational friends are another great type of friend to have around. I've heard others refer to these are proximity friends. These friends are purely your friends because you are in similar situations or places. For example, I have work friends. I love them, they make the work day so much better, but we wouldn't have ever known each other if it wasn't for landing in the same work environment.

I had MANY people that were friends because we were in the same class. In college you tend to get quite close to others in your same major. You take many of the same classes and have many consistent fears. Because of this close proximity it just makes sense to be friends. Some of my absolute closest friends were college situational friends. We would study together, share notes, and spent time laughing about ridiculous things while waiting for our next class. One of my close situational friends I even work with today. But we aren't close anymore. We both are different people and live our lives in different ways. We were simply friends because it was convenient.

You can't be friends with someone without spending time with one another. This only gets harder the older you get because time is hard to come by. When you have people already built into your daily work or school, it's easy to put in the time it takes to build a friendship. Sometimes, these friendships can blossom into real, deep, lifetime friends, but many times, when one person moves on or changes the situation, the friendship gradually fades away. I can't tell you how many work friends I have had that I was incredibly sad when they got new jobs. Not because I wasn't happy for them but I knew it marked the end of our relationship the way it was. Yes, we would meet for dinner a couple of times here or there, but eventually, we would fade into our lives, pulled away into survival mode.

These types of friends are crucial to getting through and even thriving in your day-to-day life. These are the people who hear your daily vents or daily excitement. I would say, on the surface, these friends make the largest impact on how your every day plays out. I was working at a bank when I was going through the hell that was the month or two leading up to my divorce. I wasn't sure what to do, how I was going to handle my life, or even what steps to take. I had a group of three friends who worked every day with me from 7 am to late afternoon. They were the ones who heard the vents and even cries some days. They asked me challenging questions, assured me it would be okay, and even made ways for me to move forward.

I walked into work one Saturday morning, with all new clothes from Walmart complete with the blistered feet from cheap shoes. I had left my house the night before for safety concerns and stayed in a cheap hotel without any of my things. They jumped into friendship mode. They made sure I had a place to stay for the following month and clothes that would enable me to continue working. I honestly have no idea what I would have done or where I would be now without these amazing ladies helping me in that situation. They were there each and every day to help and guide me. But the moment I moved back home three hours away, the friendship was done. Don't get me wrong, I would still do anything to help them if they needed me and vice versa, but without our built-in time together, our friendship was done.

These friends are SO important to have. They are put in your life for a specific reason and purpose—as are YOU to many people as well. They are the ones to help you when everyone else disappears. They make the daily grind of life purposeful and, yes, even fun sometimes!

The sucky part of these friendships is that since they are situational, there is an end. Yes, once in a while, you may be able to hold onto someone new, but most of these friendships die out after a couple of dinners to catch up. Eventually, you both merge into your new roles and are afterthoughts.

The important part of these relationships is to treasure what they are, when they are. Enjoy each day you are able to be close to this person, and make sure it's a two-way street. Give them the same love and amusement you get from them. Check in with them and, most importantly, ASK about their lives. Take an interest! During this specific time in my life, not only were they helping me decide what to do, but I got to know them and their families. I could tell you about their amazing kids, the special events they had, and the things they were going through as well. The worst you can be with a situational friend is to be a selfish one. I always tell my daughter conversations take two people. When someone asks you about something ask them too. Be authentically interested in your situational friends. You will learn a lot and love them for the entire time you are blessed with their friendship.

Once a while, you will have a situational friend turn into a lifetime friend. One of my favorite people in this world started out as a situational friend. Mikaela and I met for the first time at a new teacher professional development day. I knew from the moment she talked during our ridiculous "get to know you" game we would be instant friends. Over the next couple of years, we grew a true lifetime friendship. We were both in each other's weddings and I CANNOT imagine not being friends with her for the rest of my life. While most situational friends are just that, situational, be open to what could evolve.

Lifetime Friends

Let me introduce you to four of the most amazing people on planet Earth. Sarah is the first one. She is a year older than me and we have LITERALLY been friends since I was born. Attending my mother's daycare, Sarah and I have been through anything you can imagine. We grew up, went to dances together, attended each other's family holidays, and have been there without a moment's notice DESPITE being three hours away from each other.

The next one is Sara. (Yes, Sara was a very popular name in the late 80's) I was lucky enough to have her as a situational friend in the fifth grade. Her parents had recently moved to my town, and by the grace of God, we were put into Mrs. Smith's class. By default, we were instant friends. Sleepovers and activities lined up until we had officially moved into real, lifetime friends. This friendship has been the purest of pure since that day. She is the friend who tells you what you need to hear even if it's hard to say because she loves you.

The third and fourth ones I will lump together. When I was ten I received a call that would change my entire life in the best way possible. Late on a cold January evening, my mom answered our landline phone to a man named Pat. He and his friend Craig, were starting up a traveling softball team and wanted to know if I would be interested in playing. From that day forward, softball would be life. What I wasn't aware of at the time, is each of these men, who were my adopted dads, had daughters who would grow to be the greatest friends of all time. Amanda and I were instantly close, sharing a position and more hotel rooms than I can remember. Ashlee was a teammate who, once we entered into high school years, saw how much we had in common and built a strong relationship. Both of these girls have turned into lifelong friends.

The common denominator all of these girls share is no matter what, they stayed. Like I admitted in the self-esteem portion, I was insecure and weird beyond measure. I'm sure I wasn't very easy to be friends with at times. But despite the crazy and the bad decisions these friends chose to STAY. They decided to stick around and show love even when it was hard. I chose to stay too. Like all young people, they were weird and crazy in their own way but I didn't leave them either. We chose to stay and fight through the rough times in order to hang onto what we had in each other.

So how did we all stay close? What was different making them lifelong friends? I believe a huge factor was how we gave each other space and permission to grow. Thank the Lord, I am not the person I was when I was 10. Or 16 or even 25. We are supposed to grow and change but that doesn't just affect us as an individual but all the people around us. Some friendships are situational in the era they are present for. But once one person grows or reaches a new phase of life, the friendship just doesn't work anymore.

My group of friends was awesome at allowing space and growing together. This doesn't mean we were always at the same stages or even currently at the same life stage. I had been married, had my daughter, and been divorced before many of them had been married. This says more about my poor choices, but the point is that we weren't always at the same point in our lives. Many times, I felt they didn't understand what I was going through, nor did I understand what they were going through. But what kept us together is caring enough to empathize and help where we could.

College is a weird time with old friends. Three of my friends all attended the same state school respectively, while I was off chasing collegiate sports. There were many times I felt left out but only because of where I was. The group who was together didn't always spend their time together either. Your college days are such a time of exploring and growth and you MUST give your friends time to explore and take time to grow yourself. You can't be glued to your past while trying to grow into your future. There would be weeks at a time when we didn't talk or maybe only sent a quick text to check up with each other. But this was OKAY! We would always find time during a long weekend home or summer off to spend quality time and catch up. It was during these times I got to see and experience the amazing people my friends were evolving into. You must grow and choose to love and be committed friends throughout all stages of your life. This makes long-lasting BFFs.

Honesty is another extremely hard attribute of TRUE and RAW friendship. My girl Sara, without an h, is the realest and most spot on friend I have. There have been many times I haven't loved hearing her advice or agreed with her points about everything but it took REAL love and friendship to say those things. DO NOT be the yes friend all the time. There is supporting your friends, and then there is guiding your friends. I WISH someone would have been honest and smacked me when I was getting married for the first time. Everyone tells you their opinions AFTER the fact. I'm sure I still would have gone through with it but at least it would have been out there. Let me tell you. It takes a REAL friend to be straight and honest. Do you think your friend likes telling you, "Hey, you are being an idiot!" No. It hurts them. It's hard to be that real, but when a friend chooses to be uncomfortable for the betterment and care of you, it is beyond real, raw friendship.

The final piece of the BFF puzzle is grace, grace, and more grace. I've been friends with these people for up to 35 years! There are beautiful stories out there about 70 and 80-year-old friendships. Do you think they stayed friends because they are just that perfect for each other? NO! They have shown grace over and over again. There are times when just a cranky morning remark can set a confrontation in motion. Other times it may feel like your friends have abandoned you.

When I was going through my divorce, I had never felt more

alone. I felt like everyone disappeared and I had to go through it without my best friends. While this was not entirely true, it was what I felt at that present moment. The reality, is it was such a big event people didn't know how to handle it or what to say. (More on this in my book about divorce).

There will be times you or a friend's life changes in a BIG way. Maybe you move, or they get married, or you both start a new career. After a few months, it may feel like no one cares. Like everyone moved on with their lives. While the rebuttal to this is they DID move on, they had to, it doesn't change how you are feeling. I'm sure each of my friends has their own example of this. The point is that we chose to extend grace. We CHOSE to empathize with where the other person was at the moment, forgive, and move on. There is no limit to grace. You must keep giving grace as much as you need grace yourself.

While these are just a couple of examples I remember off the top of my head, can you imagine the times I don't even know about? The times I hurt their feelings or wasn't there for them? The number of times I put a boy in front of them or wasn't there in the right way to have their back? But that's the point. They extended grace without me having to request it. Being a lifelong friend means extending grace when the other person doesn't even know something's wrong.

The most important thing I can teach you about life is that we all suck. Each and every one of us. We wake up each day and try our best to suck a little less than we did the day before. If you can remember this with yourself, your friends, and really anyone you encounter, it's crazy how much more grace you will extend. We all need grace. Practice giving grace freely to all your friends.

Evolution of Friendships

With all these different types of friendships, it is important to point out that friendships evolve and change. People evolve and change. Situations evolve and change. While many types are situational by design others will change and adapt. Some of my greatest friends began as situational friends. Others were BFF's until we both realized we weren't good for each other anymore. What's important is to take a look at your friendships and analyze how they are going. There are some friendships that need to end. Others, you may find yourself wanting to form a deeper and more real friendship. All of these situations are okay! The biggest thing to remember here is to be thankful for the time you had. Be grateful for what it was and release it. There doesn't need to be a huge fight or social media announcement-just love and release.

This year my daughter was sick for a week. While she was gone, her group of friends decided to kick her out of their ten-year-long friendship group for who knows why: something dramatic and 10-year-old-like. While it wasn't the idea of them not wanting to be friends that made me mad. It was the delivery. The first day my daughter was back was a Friday. During their last recess, they teamed up and told her they didn't want to be friends anymore, right as the whistle sounded, and they were expected to run back into school and soon be dismissed for the weekend. My daughter was a WRECK! And I was PISSED! If you don't want to be friends with someone anymore, that is fine-healthy even! But there is never a reason to purposely hurt someone. Especially with people who you have loved and cared about.

The year before, my daughter had pulled the same thing with a friend in her class. She didn't like what the girl talked about and decided she didn't need to be friends anymore. She landed herself in the counselor's office after spouting off to this surprised little girl, she was no longer friends with her. That night, we had a lengthy conversation about how to not be friends with someone and how to handle it. Or more importantly, how NOT to handle it.

While these are everyday elementary school examples, it is still a problem with adults. Just because I no longer had a friendship with a coworker doesn't mean I went behind her back talking trash and being terrible. THERE IS ZERO NEED FOR THAT!!! It truly says more about the person doing it than about the person of interest. Love your friendships for what they are, when they are. And if the time comes for your friendship to end for whatever reason, love that person enough to let it go respectfully.

BEING A GREAT FRIEND

While we've talked about a lot of different parts of friendship, it really comes down to just being a good friend. A good friend acts in very certain ways and is worth putting time and energy into.

Make Time

Make the time. Find time to invest in your friends. Although I mentioned many times previously, there are moments when your lives will be in different stages, an effort to make time still needs to be a priority. Sometimes that's just a text a week checking in with each other. Other times it's making sure you have lunch together. The point isn't how much time or even what you are doing but that you care enough to at least TRY to make each other a priority.

Trust me. When you are all trying to figure out a day to meet for dinner after months of doing life you don't want to be the person who is always busy. People have time. It's just not a priority. Make your friendships a priority.

Support Each Other's Growth

There shouldn't be anyone else who is a bigger fan of you than your friends. If your circle isn't clapping the loudest for your success, then you need a new circle. There should never be a moment in your mind where you are wondering what your best friends think about you. I have some of the most badass friends in this world! One is the CEO of Apple, one is a life-saving doctor, another is the leader of The Great Teacher Revolution, and another is the owner of Perkins. Although their titles may actually be slightly different, it doesn't change the way I see them. There is no one better!!!! I am sooooo beyond proud of everything they are and do. Because besides their careers, they are the most loving and generous people on this planet. Your friends should be the first ones to celebrate and point out just how amazing you are! Being a good friend means being one of their biggest fans!

Forgive

Forgive, forgive, forgive. Remember we all suck. Your real friends realize you suck and point it out at times, but give you the forgiveness and love to move on. Choose to forgive. Choose to be the one that stays. Your friends won't be perfect. Don't put that on them. Love them for who they are and where they are. Never stop forgiving.

Know Their Love Language

This is a rather new one to me. I didn't first hear about the concept of love languages until I was in my first marriage. The original idea came from a book by Gary Chapman in which he lumps everyone into five different love languages. While I don't think it's always that clear-cut, the sentiment is still there. Know how your friends feel appreciated.

One of my best friends during my first marriage was having a really hard time in life. I was trying to make her feel better by bringing her flowers and a drink to work. It was only a few days later that she verbalized she didn't feel supported by me. I was, of course, completely surprised because I thought I was. But the way I was showing my love and support wasn't her love language. It's as if I was paying her in dollars, but she only took euros.

Know what your friends need to feel supported. Know when they need to talk versus just being left alone for a while. For some people, a heartfelt note is all they need to feel loved and supported, whereas for me- bring me a fountain Coke Zero during a challenging time, and I will break down in tears. Know your friends. It's so important.

THINGS FRIENDS NEVER DO

There are some things that friends simply SHOULD NOT ever do. Period. The end. I would like to say these are rules for all humans but again, we all suck and aren't perfect. While grace is real and should be freely given, these things you should simply never do towards ANY of your friends. A true friend NEVER:

Talks Behind Their Backs

Is there anything worse than getting up from a table and wondering if they are talking about you? Even with a healthy self-esteem, it's still awful. Your friends should never have to worry about what you are saying when they aren't there. They should be the ones standing up for you if someone else tries to do this. If you have a problem with a friend take it to THEM. Be real and raw enough to talk about it. Don't go to others talking about what is wrong.

Care about your friend enough to be real.

Holds Back Honest Advice

This is a hard one. Like I mentioned before a real friend DOES NOT hold back real and heartfelt advice. Even when it's hard, a true friend lets a person know if their boyfriend is cheating on them or simply being awful. They are direct when asking about their friend's eating disorder. A true friend doesn't simply watch their friend crash and burn in whatever way at that moment. They give warnings and advice from a loving and caring place, EVEN IF the friend doesn't want to hear it at that moment. Be willing to be loving and direct. Don't hold things back.

Let Things Build

Extending from number two, a real friend doesn't let little things build up. Wait time is important and needed for some people and situations. But if your friend ALWAYS has to pick where you eat out and it bothers you, don't let it become a thing you hold against them. What happens is that person doesn't even realize they are doing something to you, and you add a little bit of fuel each time they choose Wendy's over McDonald's. After a couple of years, it has turned into a frustration waiting to blow up. Just be honest and real about things that bother you. Talk about them before they turn into disasters.

Abandon When Things Get Hard

A true friend sticks with you no matter what. You are choosing to show up and work through the crap. When things get uncomfortable or hard they choose to stay. Remember when talking about BFF's? The difference is they chose to stay. When you were being an idiot, underage drinking, and being rebellious, they didn't join but were still there to catch you when you were down. DO NOT ABANDON YOUR FRIENDS DURING HARD TIMES! Be the one that stays. Be the one that says, We've got this and dig in with them.

CONCLUSION: BE A GIRL'S GIRL

Finally, be a girl's girl. If you haven't heard this phrase, it means to be a friend to ALL women! When a girl walks into the store with food stuck in her teeth, politely let her know. A girl walked through Target the other day with her leggings inside out, tag hanging out and all! Politely, another girl let her in on the secret. This is never to embarrass someone but to let them know. We MUST be there for each other! Some of the greatest acts of "being a girl's girl" are for safety reasons. If you see a woman feeling uncomfortable for whatever reason: a guy won't leave them alone, they look like they are being controlled, you watch someone put something in their drink, be the one to take action! Go up to them and pretend you are friends. The amount of times this has saved women is endless.

Being a girl's girl also means cheering each other on. There is room for all of us to be successful. When another woman excels at something we ALL win. There is NO power in bringing another woman down. When one succeeds, we all do. Be the girl who adjusts another woman's crown, WHILE still rocking yours.

Be a friend to ALL women! We are in this together!!!

Dating

Every day in high schools around America students have a time called Advisory. This is similar to the old homeroom or study hall. It really doesn't serve much purpose besides housing students while other groups are frantically slamming down lunch. The absolute best part of this time for a teacher is the small group of kids we get to know over the four years they attend our advisory.

Along with my core 20 students, I have many others who find their way into my room each and every day. Each one of them pulls up a stool and hovers around my desk. The first couple of times a new student joins, they are hesitant and sit a ways off. After a week or so, the feet are on my desk, food out, ready to chat. Honestly, if someone did something in the other part of the room I would have no idea. It's in these moments where magic happens. These crazy kids confined everything in me. I mean EVERYTHING. Multiple times I have had to remind them about boundaries. I coach them through anything and everything you can imagine. I am basically their life coach. While the topics are as diverse as they are, the main topic is ALWAYS dating. Girls want to know what they should say or how to act or even when to "snap" back a guy they are talking to. While I don't give them all the answers because I don't think anyone should be "snapping" when you can just text, I have accumulated quite the advice.

To some people's disappointment, this book is not going to tell you to stay away from dating. To kiss dating goodbye! To never look at a guy or think about anything your body is signaling you when walking by the most beautiful human imaginable. No. Not me. If you want a book that tells you that there are PLENTY of them out there! Trust me I grew up reading them. They all said the same; Don't date until you find the man you are going to marry. Don't make the first move. Don't have sex. These were the ONLY pieces of advice I could ever get out of the mountains of books I purchased or inherited from my youth group.

And, okay. I get it. I really do. I believe the Bible gives us some pretty clear perimeters when it comes to sexual relations. And those books are great for the few people that make it through all temptations and urges to date. But that is not the majority of us. I'm so tired of teaching to just "not do it" and moving on. All whilst we wonder why we have no idea what to do or how to handle dating situations. I'm not going to sugarcoat anything for you. Yes. Waiting to have sex until marriage is ideal, holy, admirable even. But what about the rest of us? It's time to talk about the real STUFF.

We all have different experiences and ideas about dating and I'm not here to tell you there is one clear road to take. I WISH there was a simple ten-step plan that would guarantee you find true love and make perfect life decisions, but I think this topic is personal to all of us. We all have different pasts and multiple options for the future. So instead of giving you the how-to step by step, I'm going to give ten rules I have noticed and given to all my life coach attendees. While I don't know your specific situation, I PROMISE these ten rules of dating will help you.

RULE #1: BE TRUE TO YOURSELF

When you get divorced, people have no idea what to say. They say the dumbest and most ridiculous things, but one thing people always want to know, whether it's their business or not, is why?

What happened? While I'll save the gritty details for my book on divorce, I will let you in on this secret.

The answer to what happened in my divorce was... lots of things. But looking back now there was one huge factor on my end. I wasn't true to myself. Like I shared during the self-esteem section, while I was dating and searching out my first husband I was being a person I THOUGHT I needed to be. I had tried for so many years to become the person I thought I was: a quiet little wife. And man did I play the role well. I tried and tried and really had many people convinced. I was married to my first husband for seven years, and for most of that time, I truly think I was portraying this person.

Three years into my masterful facade was the first time I tried to leave. While that story is for another day, it wasn't until year seven that I was finally free. The main reason was that I had spent seven years developing and becoming the person I was always meant to be. I was unbecoming. Day after day I was stripping off the expectations and persona I thought I needed to be. Honestly, after seven years of it, I was just exhausted. It got to a point where the thought of going one more day as this other person made me truly want to die. And I don't say that lightly! I was constantly chasing off suicidal thoughts while driving down large interstates.

As I look back over my dating years, I can see this being a pattern. Although, it wasn't always in the same form nor as serious as marriage, I can see a repeat of actions. Relationship after relationship I would be so worried about keeping them or becoming the "person" they wanted that I changed everything about who I was. If they liked golf, I was going to learn and love golf. If they were all about racing I was there being the biggest fan designing the next season's shirt. I was so eager to be the perfect fit for them. By losing myself, I became exactly what they wanted. But, after a while, either they got bored or I did. More than not, they got bored with dating themselves and broke it off. Being trapped in something as permanent as marriage, forced me to eventually figure out what I was doing. I was tired of being someone I wasn't.

I cannot express to you enough to be TRUE to yourself! Don't pretend to like football if you could not care less. Don't go back to school and study to be a business executive if all you want is to be an artist. Be true to who YOU are! Like we talked about in the first chapter, you may not always know who you are exactly or who you are in this moment. But I firmly believe you know what you AREN'T. Even while you are exploring what you love and who you are, you can be true to what your inner self is telling you. Stop pretending you are something you aren't. It will only make you miserable and hurt other people. If you are in the middle of a relationship and suddenly realize you have changed and no longer align with the person you are dating, don't feel like you must stay. People grow! It's a good thing! But many times, we outgrow a relationship or situation we are currently in. You need to adjust.

And come on, why would you want to be anything other than YOU? There is no Freaky Friday potion to switch lives with anyone so don't waste your time thinking about it. Remember in self-esteem? You are the absolute EXACT person you were made to be! Life is too short to spend time staring at a TV playing hours of Minecraft if gaming sounds like hell to you. Move on and do something you DO enjoy. Or better yet, try something new and see how you feel. Being true to who you are and who you are becoming is one of the greatest gifts you can do for yourself, the people around you, and this crazy world we live in.

BONUS TIP: I have watched thousands of girls come through the hallways of middle school and high school. I've sat back and watched to see who were the "popular" girls versus the loaners. I've watched who was labeled "attractive" and who was ignored. The difference wasn't the brand of jeans they were wearing or how much Lululemon they owned. The SINGLE characteristic every single one of the "in" girls have is confidence. They are confident in who they are! They do not care what others think or say about them because they KNOW they are great. They carry themselves with confidence. Being confident is the most attractive attribute you can have. If you want to have an endless amount of suitors, it lies in confidence in being YOURSELF!

#2: STOP TRYING TO MARRY EVERY PERSON

One cold Kansas morning, I dragged myself to early morning math help, after a 6 am dance practice. I was in desperate need of some extra help with calculus. In the brief 20-minute window before I needed to be in 1st hour, I sat quietly at a table in the back of the room with a handful of other students all begging to understand the made-up mathematical concept. It had only been a few seconds after I got out my book and notes before I began a silent (tried at least), sob. Not being able to control myself, I finally gave up on the math assignment, packed up my things, and headed out of the room. Later I would find out everyone in the room was a little surprised at just how important getting this math assignment done was for me.

I will never forget this morning. I genuinely could not stop the sobs from seeping out of my chest. No, I didn't care that much about Calculus. While I wanted to understand the assignment, I can tell you now my understanding of the insane concept was already washed from my brain. In reality, I was a 17-year-old sobbing because I truly believed my entire life was crumbling. My marriage (which hadn't even begun yet) was failing, and I was desperate to hold onto it. Yes, I write this to sound a little silly but it is 100% true! I dated a guy throughout high school and just KNEW he was going to be the one I would marry. He was my prince, my everything. And I had the tiny banded, princess-cut rock to prove it.

Guys, I was 17! Can you imagine marrying the person you were with when you were 17? I didn't know who I was let alone what I wanted in life. This was not a one-time thing either. Remember, I was fully convinced I was going to marry the tall red-headed I dated in 7th and 8th grade too. This proved to be a pattern in my dating over and over again. While a small percentage of people marry their high school sweethearts AND go on to live peaceful lives, most of us won't.

In case someone needs to tell you, YOU ARE NOT GOING TO MARRY EVERY PERSON YOU DATE! SO STOP TRYING! I know we would all like to believe we will fall in love with our person right away and live happier ever after but come on! Even the most iconic Disney princesses had to undergo SOME struggle! The odds are that you will not marry the first person you date, and we need to stop trying to. The sooner we accept this the sooner we can adapt and move on. Most of us need to fall, hurt, and get hurt until we are ready to even begin being with another person. Now, add that same reality to the other person, and you may be waiting a while. Most of us are going to date many people throughout our lives. While you are in the process of dating, you must keep this in mind.

While I'm not advocating for you to go around dating person after person without any regard for other people's feelings, I AM telling you to read the room. Where are you in life? What should your mindset be going into a relationship? As a teenager, I didn't need to be looking for a husband. What I needed was to be focused on figuring out who I was. If you are in this stage of life, go into the relationship knowing it will MOST likely end. What can you BOTH learn from each other? This is a time to figure out what you like, and what you won't ever settle for again.

Something I didn't think about until I was dating post-divorce is that this should be a time to discover how your childhood has affected the way you see relationships. Because of things we talked about in the family section, I CANNOT be yelled at. Or around. Or in the same zip code. My entire body will go into fight or flight and shut down. I had no idea this was a thing until I was in a relationship where all disagreements were met with a loud and hard reaction. It took me a while to figure out just what was happening, but once I learned I couldn't be with someone who reacted like this, I was able to move forward.

My amazing husband, now, is the softest and gentlest person, even when he's mad. I had to figure out how my trauma aligned with other people in order to know what I needed in a marriage. How do you envision relationships? How do you handle conflict? Use this time of dating to figure out how you handle situations and what brings out the best or worst in you.

Like I mentioned in rule #1, I was so caught up in marrying every person I dated that I would do whatever I needed to do to keep them. I would change my preferences and likes. This was ALL in the name of trying to marry every person; even if I didn't understand this at the time. I see so many students who stay in relationships that aren't healthy just because inwardly, they think they must make it work. Guys, it's not supposed to be that hard while you are dating. It's not supposed to be that hard period, but that's a different book as well. If you are constantly trying to fix or mediate your relationship and you are just dating, you need to ask yourself some deeper questions.

Finally, once you understand you aren't going to marry every person you date, you need to be open and honest about your intentions. Just like when I was a single mom dating in my thirties, I was VERY upfront I was not playing games and wouldn't date unless you were my person. I didn't have time or energy to waste entertaining people just for fun. The same goes for the younger years of your life. Be honest, are you in it to have fun and learn about yourself? Or are you in a phase of life where you want to be serious? Make sure the person you are entertaining is on the same page. Zero promises of the future. Be respectful of that person's time and feelings, and if something starts to change, be honest with them. And I hope both of you remember that every single relationship will end until the one that doesn't.

#3: HEAL FROM WHAT HURTS

The biggest heartbreak of my life wasn't from my first husband or even the guy I was engaged to out of high school. No, my biggest earth-shattering heartbreak was from a guy in college I had dated for two months. TWO MONTHS y'all! And it wasn't because he had the looks or money of Ryan Reynolds. He was average at best.

But like I mentioned before, I dated my best friend's cousin for three years, almost the entirety of my high school days. We were engaged during the Christmas break of my senior year. His enlistment in the military made this connection much stronger than a typical high school fling. Two weeks after we started dating he was shipped off to boot camp. He went on multiple deployments over the three years, and at the end of the relationship, we were just... done. No follow-up or awkward encounters. No missed dates or canceled plans. I didn't have to see him or learn to live without him. As sad as I was, it didn't affect my daily life. I was able to simply block it out (something I have extensive practice at) and move on. As great as that sounds to some people, I didn't heal what hurt. I ignored it all and moved on. But it was not over.

On my first day at college, I trucked in with one mission: find a baseball boy to begin a lifelong romance that ended with athletic babies. That Fall I found just that and began dating one of the only three baseball players who wore their pants correctly. (If you know, you know). Two months later, a random text message over Christmas break ended it. I was DESTROYED! You would have thought I was just broken up with by someone I had been married to for 30 years. It BROKE ME. I spent my entire Christmas break sobbing on my bed while watching hours and hours of Friends.

I got so low at one point that I group-messaged everyone in our small college community that I was emotionally dying, and I would appreciate it if they didn't bring him up at all when we got back to school. This is sooooo cringeworthy. Don't do this guys. If you ever sit down to write a group message about how broken you are just stop. Throw your phone out the window and abort. Nothing good can come from that.

The reason my whole world crashed had nothing to do with him. Yes, we had a great time for two months, but later on in life, I would realize nothing about that sadness had to do with him. I was forced to confront ALL my pain from my high school relationship. I could no longer hide from the hurt and expectation of what I thought my life would look like. I never healed from the hurt. I never allowed myself to feel the pain and sort through the meaning before moving on and simply replacing him. That poor baseball boy. He must have thought he was one day away from being a Netflix documentary. I was dealing with emotions and pain beyond my scope to handle, and none of that was his fault.

In my thirties, I see this a lot. Unfortunately, many of my social network friends are getting divorced or separating from long-term relationships. I guess it's the season of life for our bad decisions from our twenties to catch up with us. Within a week or two, many of them have already begun posting pictures about being in love or how great their new person is. While I'd like to say I'm not here to judge anyone I have to be honest: EVERYONE is judging you when you do things like this! Everyone is watching what you put out. Everyone can see how you aren't healing and just jumping into another distraction to make yourself feel better.

When I was younger, I used to give the advice the best way to get over someone was to go out with someone else. I was naive and young, obviously. This is not good advice! Yes, it is so much more fun. Especially after you have been in a relationship for a while that was obviously struggling, it brings a whole flood of fun and thrilling emotions to be wooed by a new suitor. Who doesn't love going out for free meals and being told how great they are? But this is nothing but a distraction. Eventually, the shine will wear off, and you will be left with the same heartache you needed to work through before it all started. What's worse, you will have added pain or stress from the new distraction.

It sucks. I get it. But YOU must give yourself the time and resources to heal what hurts. It is NOT your fault it all happened, but it IS your responsibility to heal before your cut bleeds on someone else. Let me tell you too, nothing is harder to watch than kids who are dealing with the revolving door of parental dating. If you are healing and have kids you MUST keep your kids as your priority. Dating after divorce is a whole other entity. But it all still boils down to healing your hurt.

#4: DON'T COMPARE YOUR JOURNEY

There are 7.8 billion people in this world. Every single one of us is completely unique and will live out an entirely different story. While we are okay with accepting we won't all have the same jobs or travel to the same places, we sure aren't okay with our dating stories being unique. I mean, obviously it's from traditions in the past but come on, it's not the 1900's! We are not glued to what our forefathers and mothers did when sweet Uncle Roy made a trade arrangement for your aunt's hand in marriage. You are allowed to have a different story. We ALL will have different stories. Because of this, STOP comparing your journey to ANYONE else's. Maybe it's your older sibling, your best friend, or some random girl on social media but you WILL NOT have their same story. You will date more/less people, and have a completely different experience.

I firmly believe there are different types of people in the world when it comes to dating. There is Girl #1, let's call her Val, who finds her love at an early age, and everything is fine. She is already mature and has gone through what she needs to go through to be with her person, and so has her partner. These people are READY for their long-term relationship. Anything they still have to learn can be done together.

Then there is Sal. Sal has a lot of weird trauma and issues she needs to work through but doesn't really know it yet. She will date multiple people and go through lots of relationships and situations that will enable her to grow into the person she needs to be when her person finally comes along. If she found her person too early, she wouldn't be the person she needed to be in a healthy relationship.

Lastly, there is Cal. Cal is the one who doesn't date anyone for quite a long time. Maybe there are a few relationships here or there but nothing serious. Cal is the girl who is 35 and longing to be married and have a family. Many times the loneliness gets to them and they begin longing for what other people have. Here's the thing about Cals. Cals are some of the GREATEST people I have EVER known in my life! They are so freaking awesome that I believe God is still trying to get their partner developed enough to be with them.

Recently, one of the Cal's in my life got married. You could tell for years she longed for a deep marriage but she refused to lower her standards. (RIGHTFULLY SO!). Day in and day out she kept being amazing and growing herself until her person finally came into her life. I know for a FACT she would not change the way it happened now. She is so happy, and both of them have come together at the right time.

Every single one of you has a different situation. You have different traumas and strengths. You have a different idea of life and dating and how it should go. Whatever your journey is, it's YOURS! I know how hard that can be sometimes when your family or friends are asking you each time you come home when you are going to get married or start having kids. While this is none of their business, most of them are genuinely coming from a good place. And even if they aren't, it is only YOU and the Lord who get to dictate the timing of these things.

I was pregnant out of wedlock and divorced by the time I was 30. This was definitely not the way my family thought my life would go and it would have been REALLY easy to compare my situation to others my age and really make myself feel terrible. Honestly, there were days I wanted to. But now I am so thankful for all I've gone through in my dating life. I have an amazing partner NOW, because of everything else I went through THEN.

Stop comparing your journey and freaking be patient!!! Lean

into your struggle and growth and allow God to take you where He wants. I promise you, it's worth it.

#5 BELIEVE IN YOUR WORTH

I spend more time on Pinterest than any other form of social media. I use it to keep my mind in check and continue to stay motivated. When I'm working on a fitness goal I load up boards with outfits I want to wear, workouts to do, and even people living fit lifestyles. I get so motivated!!! One of my favorite items to sort endlessly through are quotes. If you haven't tried this when you are struggling, go do it. Search for a topic or goal you are looking to accomplish and sift through a million different quotes waiting to inspire you.

While most quotes I love enough to pin or even download to my camera roll, there is one that sends me through the roof. I mean, I can feel every part of my skin peeling off and my annoyance and anger bursting through each and every pore. These quotes are always the same. They have some girly color or woman in the background and, in some script font across the center, state "Know Your Worth" with a heart or star shooting across the board.

Know your worth. Okay. Sure. I get it. This is what my generation has been bombarded with since we were little. You are worthy! Know your worth! I can't count how many shirts I had in my childhood chest of drawers with some version of this saying. But let's think about this. Don't you think if we could just turn on a switch or snap our focus and "Know Our Worth" we would have done so by now? Don't you think if someone telling us we are pretty, smart, or worthwhile would work, we wouldn't have spent years desperately looking for someone to love and assure us? We would love to "know our worth" but it's not that simple.

Instead, we are going to say you need to BELIEVE in your worth. Believing and knowing are completely different. Satan knew about Jesus but he didn't serve and follow him. I can know about heart surgery but I sure as heck don't believe I could complete successful surgery on someone. So instead of telling you to know your worth, I want to slap you and tell you to BELIEVE your worth!

People aren't feeding you a line. When someone gives you a compliment they mean it. We are all so obsessed with our own lives when we are telling you how great you are, WE MEAN IT! Teachers, parents, friends, coaches, all of us are WAY too busy to lie to you. But we can tell you over and over again how great and wonderful you are but until you decide to believe it, it won't make a difference. You MUST believe you have worth and then act accordingly.

Believing in your worth means having standards. It means not allowing friends to backstab you or take advantage of you. Believing in your worth means demanding a man treat you correctly. And if he doesn't? SEE YA! You must believe you are worthy to be treated correctly, to be loved and respected.

WE DO NOT BEG FOR BASIC THINGS!!! YOU DO NOT BEG SOMEONE TO GIVE YOU RESPECT AND TO BE TREATED LIKE A HUMAN BEING! You do not beg for attention or affection. We do NOT settle for someone cussing at us. We do not allow someone to not talk to us for weeks at a time in the name of "not being clingy". We do NOT stop having friends or a life outside of our relationship. We do not ask for time and to be acknowledged. WE DO NOT ASK OR BEG FOR BASIC THINGS because WE ARE WORTHY!

Just today, I was having a conversation with a student in my class. I overheard her talking about her ex being in jail and the the current guy she was talking to had to get drug tested all the time because of being on probation. I can only keep quiet in my class for so long before I MUST jump in and give advice. I asked her why she was dating the same type of person over and over again.

Her response was "The lifestyle is fun!" I didn't buy it. I said, no it's not. Doing illegal things and trying not to get caught is not fun. Dating someone who is in jail is not fun. I said, you know what is fun? Dating someone with a job. Marrying someone with a credit score high enough to buy a house. Having peace in your life is fun.

The real reason this girl keeps having these relationships is because she doesn't believe she has any worth. She settles for what she thinks she can have. Why go after a guy who has his life on track when she just "knows" he won't go for a girl like her? Until she believes in her actual worth, she will keep dating the same type of people. Trust me, we will continually keep ourselves at the same level in dating (or life) until we decide we deserve more. We must DEMAND better for our lives. Don't settle for a guy who is in trouble or can't get their schoolwork turned in. Don't settle for someone who can't hold a job even though he is 25. Don't settle for someone who treats people like objects instead of the beautiful people they are. DEMAND more. Demand to be respected, loved, cared for. YOU MUST BELIEVE YOU ARE WORTHY ENOUGH FOR THESE THINGS!

Because, news flash, YOU ARE WORTHY! You are inherently worthy of everything just for being a living breathing human.

There is no length of hair or low enough weight that makes you part of the club. You are a child of God and that is all you need. You are a person. You are worthy! It doesn't matter how your parents or previous people treated you. Your worth is not dependent on anyone else. Your worth begins and ends in your mind. You must believe it. Only when you start believing this will you begin to demand the things you deserve.

#6: BREAKUP LIKE IT MATTERED

Since we have talked extensively about not marrying every person as well as believing in your self-worth we need to discuss the next rule: Break-Up like it Mattered. While I don't have extensive experience in this, the few times I did I can honestly say I didn't break up like it mattered. I dated a wonderful football player in college for three years. Because, as I have mentioned earlier, I lost myself and just wanted to like and do all the same things he did, I eventually got crazy bored. I wasn't aware of this until I was paired up with a dreamy baseball boy for a class project. While I didn't cheat, it ignited a fire inside of me I hadn't felt in years. I knew I needed to end it. But, instead of talking to him with respect and being honest, I pulled the whole, "I just need a break." Guys, no one just needs a break. This is such a cop-out.

When people avoid break ups or talk about how terrible they are, I really believe MOST of the time, it is because of how it happened. People let fear and selfishness get in the way of treating the other person like someone who has value. Remember, just like you are worthy, so is the other person. They deserve to be treated just as well as you do. This means when it's time to end things, you do it right.

For the longest time I thought I was cursed with text message breakups. Over and over again guys would text me things were over because they were cowardly punks. The whole situation doesn't feel great, but it feels even worse when you aren't respected. This is not a hard concept, no matter how complicated we try to make it.

Do it in person. I mean it. The ONLY way to break up with someone is to do it in person. This one is hard, I know, but don't argue with me. I had to break up my marriage face to face. So I PROMISE you can break up with the person you've been dating for a week face to face. The real point here is it doesn't matter how long or how deep the relationship got; every person deserves to be talked to face to face. If you are in a long-distance situation, Facetiming is always an option. In this day and age, there is zero excuse to break up with someone, NOT in person. While we are at it, no ghosting. Even if you are just talking to someone and was never official. If you have expectations of any communication you need to tell them you are done with the relationship. No ghosting. No texting. No Snapchatting, or any other social media that may have come out since this book has been published. You have this conversation FACE TO FACE.

Be direct. When you are in person talking, the next worst thing you can do is not be completely direct and honest. The things I've heard over the years are endless. "I just need a break." "Maybe we can get back together in a few days." "I'm just really busy right now." "I don't have time for a relationship." You may think these lines "soften" the blow but in reality, they give the person false hope. You are giving them just enough to hold onto so they think you might get back together. DO NOT DO THIS. Tell them it's over and leave it at that. Stop talking. FULL STOP. Respect the other person enough, to be honest and allow them to mourn and move on. When you leave a door open, even ever so slightly, you are restricting the grieving process. Be direct when it's over.

Be honest. So many times, the hardest part of a breakup is all the what-ifs. You are wondering if there was someone else, or if you did one singular thing that sent them over the edge. Take these out of their mind. Be honest about why it didn't work out. Tell them you just don't work well together. Or they are too clingy. Or you are having feelings for someone else. Whatever the reason, be honest. Again, this is clearing up all the wondering in their minds so they can then begin the process of moving on. When you are holding back information like this, you are limiting the other person's ability to grow.

Whoever you date or spend time with is worthy just because they are humans. Treat them like they are worthy and that your relationship mattered even when it's over.

#7 BE AWARE OF RED FLAGS

There are not enough pages to cover every red flag you may run into out in the wild. They aren't just a funny setup in a Vince Vaughn comedy. I'm telling you there ARE red flags and you MUST believe them. Before we jump into a few of the larger red flags let's talk about what I mean. Despite how pop culture has portrayed red flags, they are really anything that signals that a person may not be a healthy choice. It's a consistent behavior that SHOULD scream at you this person is not going to treat you or others the way you should be treated.

Unfortunately, I was the Queen of ignoring red flags. I was the Christian girl who thought I could missionary date myself into a healthy relationship. Nothing got me more excited than finding a guy who was down on himself or came from a hard family. Maybe he had a past. I blame Disney for instilling my original need for a fixer upper. The problem with this philosophy, is you should never go into a relationship HOPING to change a person. It won't happen and you shouldn't waste your time on it.

A girl in one of my classes is in an extremely toxic relationship. I have had conversation after conversation with her about the red flags. But she is convinced they are just in a "hard" spot. She has been convinced they must put in the work to get through these rough times. Guys. She's a sophomore in high school. IT SHOULDN'T BE THAT HARD!!! Even if you are an adult in a relationship, it SHOULD NOT BE THAT HARD YET! Fighting through the hard is for a couple who is married and growing apart or one of them has hurt the other. Fighting through the hard is for trying to keep a family together and being there for their kids. Fighting through the hard is NOT for someone you have been dating for a month or two. Remember Rule #2? We aren't trying to marry every person we date! When a red flag flies we take it for what it is and end the relationship. This is called dating ya'll. You MUST start seeing and believing the red flags.

Common Red Flags

Disrespect

I love my students, I really do. I have the craziest and most goobery students ever, and I love every part of them. I try really hard to allow all my students to be who they are. I always tell them at the beginning of the year I want them to be THEM. I never want them to hide their personality. But they must do it respectfully. Disrespect is truly the deepest red flag. All abuse and trauma stems from disrespect. When someone shows they are disrespectful to you or others it is a bright red flag. Someone thinking it's funny to cuss or talk down to teachers is disrespectful. Not caring enough to meet your parents or friends is disrespectful. Treating the server at Chili's terribly is disrespectful. Being mean and rude to you, even in the name of "joking," is disrespectful. If someone is disrespectful to one person, they will be to anyone. BELIEVE this red flag and get out.

Begging for Basic Things

One of my college boyfriends was a charmer. He was a baseball player, super tan, slightly crooked smile-everything needed to make my heart pound. We "talked" for an entire Spring semester (a red flag on its own), but that's not what this flag is about. This is how it ended. We ended up dating all through summer in between jobs and summer ball. In the words of T Swift, it truly was a cruel summer. Every single day I would wait for him to text or call me. Everything was on his schedule. He ignored me when he wanted to and talked to me when he was lonely. Don't get me wrong, it wasn't this clear at the time. It was always "I have a job I can't look at my phone with" or "I have practice all evening" While those sound like valid excuses, he mowed grass and listened to his phone the entire day. And even while traveling or practicing, we all know someone can check-in. Writing this now, I feel like such an idiot, but I promise it didn't feel this clear at the time.

We would hang out a couple of times a week and spend great summer evenings together. We would laugh and be super lovey. But as soon as we were back to our lives it was back to his time only. Guys, I was begging for basic things. I was begging to be a priority. I was begging to be seen. All I wanted was basic relationship actions. I wasn't being a crazy clingy whatever. And by the way, MOST of the time, guys refer to a woman as that; they are just asking for normal things. It is NORMAL to hear from the person you are dating at minimum every morning and night. Text messages take half a second people!

The night I knew it was over was when I finally gathered some respect for myself. After a long night out with another girl with zero contact, I was finally done. I was finally able to see what was really going on. GUYS! We do not beg to be a priority in someone's life. We do not beg for the attention or validation we so desperately need at times. We do not beg to be seen or be in public together. NEVER EVER play the secret partner. If you find yourself doing this, it's not meant to be. Be the one who breaks it off. Because the hard truth Sis, is if he is treating you like this, you just aren't a priority. And that isn't going to change. Do the work for him and peace out.

Trust your Gut

This flag is a little bit harder to explain. It will also get many "religious" people to cross me off their list to follow and I'm okay with that. When you are dating or even just spending time with someone you MUST learn to listen to your gut. For me, I call this listening to your soul. My entire first marriage was engulfed in daily reminders to not trust your heart but trust your brain. Okay. This is great and biblical unless you have extreme anxiety and OCD and cannot trust what your brain is saying. I've heard this contrast all my life because the heart part is truly biblical. But after years and years of hearing and trying my best to follow this, I believe it's not always so cut and dry. I feel with my heart, my brain, and most importantly, my soul. So when I say trust your gut I really mean trust your soul. For me, my soul is an entirely different feeling. My Lord and Savior resides in my soul and when I am listening to my soul I am hearing from the Holy Spirit itself-and I KNOW it's not wrong.

The purest example of this was dating after my divorce. This is when I finally broke away from the distortion that was listening to my heart or mind and learning to listen and trust what my soul was saying. I had been dating a guy for just a couple of months. Nothing too serious, but I was getting out there and exploring. He was a nice guy, truly. He treated me great, seemed to be a great dad, and had goals in his life. The problem was, every time I was around him my soul would erupt. I couldn't and still can't figure out exactly why, but any time we hung out, I was soooo uneasy. I was nervous, anxious, panicky. My mind would race a million miles a minute, and I simply could not feel at ease. Eventually, I broke it off, but despite my own advice, I truly couldn't give him a reason.

A while later, still not looking for anything super serious (honestly, I never wanted to get married again) I ended up hanging out with a man by the name of Bill. While Bill and I had been lunchroom teacher friends for a few months, nothing more had really blossomed. We both were adamant we never wanted to get married and laughed about it in the hallways. But after a day of Facebook messaging and joking we decided to see if anything more was there. Guys. That time of us sitting on the couch watching TV is a time I will NEVER forget. It was the most incredible and crazy feeling I have ever had. My soul was on fire but in a loving, almost knowing, way. It was so insane! I barely knew this man but it felt as if I was on the beach with the perfect breeze running over my face. We would talk later, he was feeling the same thing. It was like our souls were finally reconnecting after being apart for hundreds of years. It just felt right. It felt PEACEFUL. At this point in my life, all I wanted was peace. Peace for me. Peace for my daughter. Peace in life. I didn't want anything around me that would alter that peace.

This was my soul talking. This was something deeper than my heart or brain. It was the part of me that knew way before I did. That soulful feeling has never gone away with Bill, and I am now madly in love and married to this man. It has been five years and nothing has changed. I have also had many other situations since then I was able to listen to my soul and follow it. This is a skill. It has to be practiced. Listen and work on hearing it. I find the more I spend in prayer and reading scripture the clearer I can hear it.

As sweet as my love story is, this is really about the red flag. If your soul is constantly anxious and on fire when you are with someone, trust it. You don't have to make sense of it. Not everything has an answer. It may just be loud alarms going off trying to alert you to get away from this person. I firmly believe your soul talks to you in relationships as well as any other situation in your life. Learn to hear it, TRUST IT, and move accordingly.

How You Feel About Yourself

I really feel like this red flag should be easy to see and follow, but I fell victim to it, as many girls do every day. How you feel about yourself while you are with someone is extremely telling. Although we've talked about not giving that power away in our self-esteem portion, people still have an impact. Your parents have an impact. Your friends have an impact. The person you are dating has a HUGE impact. So how are you feeling about yourself since you have been a couple? Have you had a great view of yourself believing you're the amazing person you are and that you can accomplish anything you set your mind to? Or are you constantly focusing on what you need to change and how you don't add up? While these feelings could be coming from a different source, I'm telling you, you need to listen and observe this when you are in a relationship.

I've never had the self-esteem I have now. I think I'm HOT and funny and soooo freaking smart it drives me crazy most days. I have the audacity to write down ten goals I'm working on every single morning. More, I believe I can actually accomplish them! While I have put a lot of work into myself in my thirties, I'm telling you it's in large part to my husband. There is not a single second he doesn't truly believe I am the greatest and most gorgeous person in this world. Even when he's giving me honest correction or advice he is still seeing and projecting the greatest version of me to myself. It's actually insane to see.

In contrast, I've reflected back on other relationships and can see so many times where my confidence was limited because of the person I was with. Especially in my first marriage. No joke, this man had a list of things I needed to work on. How do you think that made me feel? I was always getting told what I needed to do better but never how I was capable of doing it. After a few years of this, you start to believe all the terrible things you are hearing. You believe you are the worst wife and "full of Satan". Even if it's disguised in good intentions. You MUST be aware of how you feel about yourself when you are with someone. If you constantly feel the need to change or be someone else, burn the red flag and walk out the door. The right person will want you to be your best, but have the ability to see the greatness that you are, even when you can't.

#8: SEX IS A REAL, FEMALE MONSTER

Yes. We are going to talk about the monster in the room. Sex. I will write an entire book on sex someday because I feel so insanely passionate about it. I grew up in church, like, every Sunday of my life grew up in church. Year after year all I ever heard was sex before marriage was a sin. Period. Done. Nothing else. And yes, that is biblical but we never talked about what to do if you do mess up and have sex. We talked in depth about how to stop other sins like cussing or lying. But sex was just a quick no. No explanation. We never talked about sex within a marriage and that it can be freaking amazing! There is a whole generation of people who finally had sex in their marriage and had no idea what to do or how to carry all the weight that comes with it. If it was brought up it was simply a quick, NO.

While I get that, truly I do, we aren't all going to wait until marriage no matter how pure your intentions are. It's just not going to happen. The amount of sex being had at younger and younger ages simply boggles my mind. What it really does is break my heart but again, another book. So let's talk about it. Let's talk about what happens when sex is introduced into the relationship.

The first thing to know is, contrary to the 2000's rap songs, I can sing word for word; sex IS a big deal. It IS a big monster that brings an abundance of its own problems and issues. It is not something you should take lightly. It's also not something you should EVER be pressured into. I don't care how hot or charming your boyfriend is. This is a decision up to you and your beliefs, that's it. But you must know, when you do have sex it is a BIG deal. I won't go into the science behind it but trust me-it jacks up our heads. We get weird, possessive, emotional, the list is endless. It is also something no matter how much you try, you can never take back. It has happened. There is no restart. So make sure you are ready for it. If you are a middle schooler or really even a high schooler, I'm telling you you are NOT ready for it. I know that makes me sound like an old hag but I'm telling you it's true! Sex is such a complex thing and our brains aren't even done developing at this age. Why do we think we can handle this?

I know I know….but you're different. You will be able to play it cool. Stop. You won't and you can't. So really think about it. If you have sex with this person and then they leave forever the next day are you prepared to handle that emotionally? If they would get up afterwards and tell you they had a disease would you be ready to cope with it? If you were to get pregnant (yes, after ONE TIME, it happens, TRUST ME), are you prepared to take that on? I'm telling you, as someone who has been in a place like this before, if you are able to handle all of these situations and they not bother you, you have locked your emotions up so tight you can't feel anything. This is NOT a place you want to be. This is a trauma response from pain and hurt. If you are dealing with this type of trauma then you REALLY aren't ready to be having sex and need to go work through your crap. Everyone else, is not mentally or emotionally ready enough to handle this. So keep that in mind if you proceed.

So if you haven't picked up on it yet, I did not wait until marriage. And while I won't get into all the details in this book I will talk about some of the actions that come afterwards. The biggest one is I felt the need to lie about it to everyone in my life. I didn't tell anyone and certainly didn't feel comfortable talking about it with my friends or family. Guys, any time you have to lie about something you are doing, it's a red flag. If you have to lie about doing something or being with someone you simply don't need to be doing it. Period.

Really, the reason is because the people in your life are there to help you through the hard stuff. They are there to help you navigate your actions in this crazy life. Because I wasn't able, to be honest about having sex to ANYONE, I never had anyone to talk to about the "stuff." All that emotional stuff we just talked about? That stuff. I wasn't able to talk to anyone about what to do now or how I was feeling.

I didn't feel like I had a support system to help me through it. The honest truth was I did. It wasn't that they weren't there. It was that I was so ashamed of breaking the one giant rule that I didn't want to talk to anyone about it. Again. If having sex puts you into this position you are not ready to have sex. You MUST be able to talk about it with your inner circle. Whoever that may be: mom, friends, aunt, whomever. You HAVE to be able to sort through feelings and emotions with someone.

So if you have had sex already when you are reading this, make sure you are being HONEST. Yes, when you bring it up, it may be a little uncomfortable at first, but NOTHING compared to having to keep it to yourself for years. Go find someone you can be honest with to help navigate it. Don't pretend you're tough or that it wasn't a big deal. It was. Be honest with yourself and be willing to talk about it.

The biggest reason I wish I would have been honest and talked to someone about having sex is because I NEEDED to know and fully understand one big rule. Just because I had sex once, or twice, however many times, it did NOT mean I had to do it again!!! Read that again. Just because you had sex with your boyfriend late one night does NOT mean you must mate every weekend or every time he asks. Even if you get out of the relationship, when you begin a new relationship you can set up new boundaries and not have sex. There is no rule out there that makes it a free game once you are no longer a virgin.

This may seem kinda strange to some but I'm telling you it's a thing. We put so much pressure and emphasis on not losing our virginity that once we have, there is an odd feeling that it doesn't matter anymore. You have sex without even fully thinking about it. It's almost as if it's lost the weight of the situation. Please, PLEASE hear me. Every single time you have sex, it is a big deal. Every single time you have sex with someone new, it is a big deal. It isn't like the first time you ride a bike where the fear is gone once you finally get the courage to push the peddles. When having sex, all of the very real emotions and situations are present every single time. So PLEASE. Do not feel like once you have done it, it doesn't matter. It DOES matter. And by talking to your circle and being honest about it you can help yourself see that. Since I didn't talk to anyone, I had no idea how to stop it. I allowed myself to get buried in the weight of it all until I could not feel anymore. Please, for the sake of yourself, do not let yourself get to this point.

Since this book is mainly for females we are going to tackle another sex issue that sends me through the roof: sex is NOT a man thing. Sex is NOT a man's struggle. Sex is NOT something only males care about or want. Our bodies have a natural cycle that fluctuates and impacts our urge for sex. Growing up, I always heard sex is a man issue. Porn is a man issue. Guys are the ones aroused all the time. Sex is a guy thing. Crazy, how all the people teaching or writing about these "truths" are...MEN. Sex is NOT just a male thing! In the past, it was just guys who got to have sexual urges and talk about them. But we live in the 21st century and gosh darn it, I'm going to say it: WOMEN LOVE SEX TOO! WOMEN STRUGGLE WITH SEXUAL FEELINGS TOO!

When I was first starting to have such "feelings" I really thought there was something wrong with me. I thought because I was horny and was interested in exploring things like porn and sexual education I was a complete wack job. I mean, I was a girl. Why would I be feeling like this? Girls don't feel these things. So instead of asking trusted people in my life, I hid and found myself searching for answers elsewhere. You don't want to go down that road. Believe me when I say it's normal, NATURAL, to be thinking about sex. Our bodies go through the same exact "awakening" as males do. Don't think you are broken or crazy. Find your trusted people and have the conversations you are looking for. You will have a MUCH healthier relationship with sex in the future if you do.

#9: DATING DOESN'T DEFINE YOU

Expectations. Family, friends, Disney, wherever they come from, every single day, you are bombarded with social expectations. People get married. Some do not. Some have kids. Some have dogs. Some move to the Caribbean and live a life of relaxation and harmony. All of these things are okay. More than okay, they are GREAT! But I know you getting asked about these expectations a lot, makes it really hard to hold your ground. But I promise. Be you and do you.

When your grandmother asks if you have met any nice boys while at school she is just trying to be nice. When your parents won't stop asking for grandchildren they are just excited and do not mean to put pressure on you. While I could write an entire chapter on things people should have no say or business asking or commenting on, the fact is, you will probably still get these questions. They are easy questions to ask. It's harder for your aunt to ask you about the latest bio lab you completed. It's harder for your brother to ask about your latest girl's night. It's easy to ask about the societal norms we are accustomed to.

Despite the expectations that are put on by someone else or you are mentally trapped in what Disney fed you, it is important to know DATING DOES NOT DEFINE YOU. It doesn't matter if you are 40 and not married, 23 and haven't had a boyfriend, or 30 and divorced. None of this matters. You are SOOOOO much more than who you are dating. You are so freaking interesting all by yourself. Who cares what your dating status is? Believe in how amazing you are outside of a relationship. You should be a whole person on your own and for yourself before ever getting into anything serious. Remember that. You are not defined by your relationship status. I don't care what your great-grandma says.

On the other hand, if you are in a relationship, make sure it doesn't define you either. How many times have you seen someone get deep into a relationship and lose every semblance of who they were? Have you had a friend who ignores you and forgets you are a thing while they are in a relationship? It is not healthy for your entire life to be about one thing. Especially if it's another person. I say that as a mom too! I love my daughter more than my own life but she doesn't define me. When we allow other people or distractions to define us, we lose who we really are. And remember, you are made exactly the way you are supposed to be. So stop allowing yourself to be defined by a relationship.

I was so incredibly bad at this. In middle school, after a late-night Halloween dance, I was supposed to go home with two of my friends. After a crazy night of "getting low," we had planned to talk boys all night. Instead, I canceled to go home so I wouldn't miss a phone call from my boyfriend. A PHONE CALL! Rightfully so, my friends were pissed. Make sure you have time with friends. Don't EVER allow a significant other to isolate you from your circle. Keep doing the activities you love, sports, hobbies, and clubs. Keep being YOU. Live your life as if they left tomorrow your life would still be whole. You are more than a relationship...act like it.

#10 IT'LL BE OKAY...I PROMISE

This is a broad stroke but I mean every single word. IT WILL BE

OKAY. It doesn't matter what has happened. If he cheated on you with five girls last night. If he just broke up with you after five years. If you just broke up with him because you weren't compatible. If he is just being an ass and ignoring you. No matter what it is....it gets better. 100% of the time it gets better. I can promise you this. I've been raped twice and had my heart destroyed more times than I can count but I can with 100% certainty tell you it got better...every...single...time. Even when you are hurting so bad you feel like you can't breathe, I promise it gets better. No person or situation is worth destroying your life or things in your life because of them. It doesn't matter how much pain you are feeling, it is not worth hurting yourself, quitting something, or making huge shifts in your life.

One of the best pieces of advice I've ever received was during my running era. Part of training is forcefully running many miles some of them up long and grueling hills. I was told not to ever make a decision about stopping while you are only halfway up the hill. Everyone wants to quit when they are half a mile straight uphill. You're tired, in pain, and wondering why on Earth you thought running was a good idea. But eventually.....maybe with some resources, time, or help from others, eventually you will get to the top of the hill. And your lungs will open back up, and you will catch your breath. And when you do, you'll be able to see out over the land from the top of the hill. The view from there is full of every opportunity imaginable.

I promise no relationship is worth ending it all. No relationship is worth hurting yourself. No relationship is worth giving up. IT....WILL....GET...BETTER......Don't give up while you are halfway up the hill.

Future

I'm assuming most of you readers are a part of a couple of groups. The first one is a teenager in high school trying to figure out this crazy world. At this moment you are being hit with a million life choices and options but have no idea what to choose and are terrified of "messing" it up. The other group of readers is a bit older. You are in your twenties or thirties and have lived enough life to begin asking yourself, "Is this it? Maybe you are recently divorced or have decided what you have been doing for a living for the past ten years is just not what you want. You have come here for some guidance. Regardless of which group you are in, let me start by saying-I see you. I have very much been both of these people.

I vividly remember in high school knowing I wasn't mature enough to be making lifelong decisions like what to major in or where to attend college. I've also gotten to the point in my life where something had to change. I had to reroute. I was 30, and all of a sudden, feeling like my life was starting over. I felt like I had a million options, but simultaneously, I had none at all.

Trying to plan your future is like trying to take a hound dog for a walk. You can have the clearest idea of where you are going but still be pulled from side to side. Sometimes you aren't sure why you even started out the door to begin with. The pressure is huge. The pressure is REAL! Your future decisions and plans shouldn't be taken lightly. But there are many ways I WISH I would have known to translate all the information coming at me. In all my experience of future planning, replanning, and helping students in their own pursuits, I think everything, no matter the decision, comes down to three questions:

1) What am I going to do?
2) How am I going to get there?
3) Will it be good enough?

WHAT AM I GOING TO DO?

Oh, the question we ask ourselves even more than our teachers, parents, or friends. My sweet girl's school begins every year with a picture and a writing sample of what she wants to be when she grows up. As sweet as it is when you're 10, it hits differently when you are 17 or 18, or 30 and trying to make real-life decisions. You are no longer dreaming about becoming the President of the United States or the fastest Aldi checker in the world. You are facing real, honest, and important choices.

The first thing I want you to REALLY understand is that it's OKAY not to know yet. I don't care if you are 50 and still trying things out. It's okay not to know. And more than that, it's okay to answer people when asked that you do not know. Because guys, even if you DO know, most of us are going to switch it at some point. Most people change their major at least once. And beginning with my generation, are no longer working one job for 40 years. It just doesn't happen. Most of the jobs that were available 40 years ago don't even exist anymore! Who knows how often you will have to change and adapt? So it is MORE than okay not to know what you want to do. Whether it's not knowing what you want to do next year or when you are 40. It is OKAY!

Eventually, you will have to make SOME decisions. And there are a few pieces of advice I'd love to give you. The first is to try everything. Currently, in Kansas, we have these things called pathways within our education system. For every career and technical route there is a line of classes you are supposed to take before you graduate. This is something that is preached from middle school until the day you walk across the stage in a cap and gown. I currently teach within a pathway and am the worst supporter you will find. Our extra funding is based on how many students complete a pathway. That means they have to take 6-10 classes aligning with one singular career such as health science, hospitality, or education. As great as it may look on paper, students are leaving ready to go straight to a program or career, and I'm telling you it's hurting kids. We are asking 14 and 15-year-olds to choose a pathway and stick with it. Do you think they have any idea of what they want to do? Even if they have some semblance of an idea, they don't really understand what the job entails.

When I was this age all I wanted was to be an orthodontist. So I loaded up on college math and science classes. Besides my one mandated PE class freshman year, I took ONE single elective during my entire four years of high school. And it was video editing so I could make the sports highlight videos. That's it. I never took art or yoga or any trades-nothing. I was soooo laser-focused on where I was going I didn't take the time to look up and see if it was really where I wanted to be.

Obviously, I didn't become an orthodontist. No, in my junior year of college, I decided I hated science and didn't want to continue. Guys, can you imagine how much time and energy was wasted sticking to my "pathway"? What we should be rewarding in our high schools is how many different pathways a student tries. If a student tries five different pathways within high school THEN we get extra funding. This is how they learn what they want to do and quite frankly, what they can't imagine ever doing again. High school is the safest time to do this. You can take internships, do observations, or just take an intro class and get immersed in the subject. If you don't like it, so what? The semester is only so long that you aren't out anything. Take advantage of every option you have.

If you are one of my older readers I want to encourage you to never stop learning. If you have no idea what you want to do, it's still okay. Most of us are in a spot where we need to hold a job to pay bills, but while we are doing that, we can explore. Shadow someone, take free classes online, and ask a million questions to people who are doing what you want to be doing! Your time for exploring is NOT up! We just have to get a little bit more intentional with our time and resources. We now live in a world where not only can we find out how to do ANYTHING online but we have so much information we have to sort through it in order to find out what is legit. Sometimes, this drives me crazy, but what a time to be exploring! I can try on being a doctor, dentist, teacher, or a business owner without ever leaving my amazing living room chair.

While you are trying a little bit of everything, do not be afraid to "fail". I put that in quotations because I don't believe in failure. It's all an experience. It's all part of the journey of finding what you want in this life. Be okay with something not being for you. I am 35, and the number of things I've tried is quite laughable. I've been a videographer, coach, bank teller, salesman, stay-at-home mom, gym manager, English teacher, Chinese teacher, Innovative English teacher, gifted facilitator, and now culinary teacher. These are just all the CAREER things I've tried. Not to mention the million different hobbies and lifestyles I've tried. Can you imagine how many of these I have "failed" at? Oh goodness. Most I have puddle through but I was not exceptional. Something was always lacking, but with each switch, I gained more experience and confidence in what I really wanted in life.   You aren't going to be amazing at everything and that's okay. But it ALL adds up to your skills and experiences that make you, YOU. And help you figure out what you want to be doing. I've known I've wanted to be a writer since 4th grade but how was I supposed to make that happen? My degree and experience teaching English has made me a better writer. My MBA has given me the knowledge to market my book. Everything in between helped give me the insight and examples I needed to support my message. It ALL came together for a reason.

Reality Check

A HARD future reality check I hate to break to you, is you won't necessarily be passionate about your job. My husband is part of the pessimistic Generation X. While I was raised being told I could do anything I wanted and to find what I was passionate about, he was being told life is what it is-get a job, pay the bills, and eventually die. While I think that is a very sad way to live life, his generation does seem to have fewer issues than my millennial counterparts. What has happened is by constantly being asked what we love or are passionate about, we think we aren't happy or complete until we are doing something for a living filled with said passion. Don't get me wrong. There's nothing I want more in this life than to be a full-time writer traveling and writing about matters I'm passionate about. But the odds are, MOST of us will find a career doing something that is just that-a career. It will pay for our lifestyle and provide for our families, but our day-to-day may not be about passion and dreams.

My sweet husband's father, rest his soul, always told him someone has to pick up the trash. While this is a perfectly respectable career, it paints a very true reality. For society to work, all different jobs have to be done. I'm not sure anyone is super passionate about picking up the poop at the park. Or serving up chicken patties every Wednesday to a bunch crazy students. I don't think anyone grew up desperate to be sorting through mail day end and out but all those jobs are respectable and NEEDED for our society to work.

So while I'd love to tell you everything you do for work will be filled with passion, I would be lying to you. Most of us will have a career and separate things we are passionate about. At my age, you really figure out that most of your passions or joys are the things you do outside of work. While there are things I love about my job, my passions and most joy come from who I surround myself with and the hobbies I pursue. If I get to the point someday for one of them to pay for my life, I will count myself one of the lucky ones.

So after that great piece of news where do you go? There are two questions I ask my students and would encourage you to ponder over when thinking about what you want in life. The first one is what do you want your daily life to look like? From the moment (and time) you wake up until you come back to your house what do you want your life to look like? Do you want to work alone? Do you want to be outside? Do you like transactional work where you always know you are doing it correctly? Do you need to be challenged and stimulated? Do you like being "on" all day every day? Where do you want to live? Honestly, what do you want your lunch break to look like? Do you want to have to bring your lunch every day or do you want to go out for lunch? Do you want to work from home? The day-to-day intricacies of your life are going to be what makes the daily grind joyful or not.

Currently, I'm a teacher. I wake up at 5 am, leave my house at 6:45, and begin teaching at 7:20. I work nonstop and have to be on every moment of every day. I'm around hundreds of people and share my 20 minute lunch with students needing life advice. I go home overstimulated, starving, and just need to pee! While I love my job, this is not what some people want their daily lives to look like. Ask those questions. Imagine your every single day and ask yourself what type of job plays into those strengths. I promise you, what you are selling isn't as important if you are working the hours you want, from where you want, and how you want. We are all made for different skills and environments. Do your best to figure out yours and find careers that match up.

The second question to ask is, who do you want to be around? Some people don't want to be around another soul. They want to go to their job, complete their work, and never have to interact with anyone. Others thrive by having daily conversations and building relationships with those around them. I'm telling you, the line between loving and hating my job was only five miles. I was doing the same job but the difference was the people. The individuals you do life with daily are what make a day great. This year I'm working with someone who has become one of my very best friends. We have the same sense of humor and are just huge nerds together. I guarantee there are people who would hate their jobs if they were matched with us, but we work together so great! It makes work fun and fast. So think about the people or type of person you want to work around. This can make a huge difference.

The most common fear I encounter sitting with students or even peers as they are making future decisions is that they will make the wrong decision. People get so terrified of making the wrong choice they prefer not to make one at all. I have held students in tears as they are in full panic from decision-making.

My stepchild had this same experience. They had many options when choosing a college. They could go to many places with many scholarships, but one really stood out. Yes, they wanted to go to Alaska. ALASKA! While I don't understand this, I DO understand wanting to take a challenge and make an experience out of your college years. We were in the car on the way to feast on our beloved Texas Roadhouse rolls when they were trying to make their final decision. I finally peeped in with advice I give all my students at this crossroads. I said, "Stop worrying about making the "wrong" decision. There ISN'T a wrong decision. Unless your plan is to break the law or hurt yourself or others there is NOT a wrong choice...there are just choices. You go, experience, and adapt."

For them, both colleges they had narrowed down to were great options! Both would give them a great degree and experience. I encouraged them to go to Alaska. Go experience! What's the worst that happens? You go for a semester and decide it's not for you? So what! You adapt, pivot, and have still learned so much during that semester. Every experience we have adds to our wisdom and lives. Stop trying to figure out what the RIGHT choice is. Just choose the best one at that moment and be ready to pivot.

This past summer my amazing grandmother took me to Europe. Although I saw enough amazing things to fill up my phone storage, I will always remember the statues. There are statues every single place you go. Just naked person after naked person, many times with water spewing out of some hole. While most of them didn't mean a lot to me, after looking at the hundredth one I really got to thinking.

These statues have been around for hundreds of years. You can tell where the sun and weather have beaten them down. You can see where men have tried to make them like new again. But day after day, no matter what, that statue stays there. It is permanent. Guys...you ARE NOT a statue!!! You don't have to stay in one spot! This goes for my younger and older readers. No matter where you are at, if it's horrible enough, you can leave! We no longer live in a trapped society where you may never see 10 miles outside of your town. We live in a global society that allows you to try new things and make changes any time you want. Yes, pay your bills and take care of your family. But YOU AREN'T A STATUE! Don't stay in something that is killing you. Be thankful you can pivot and change course.

Finally, when asking the question of what I am going to do, I BEG you to have some stinking confidence in yourself. While I found that I didn't like science, I still loved teeth and very much wanted to be an orthodontist. What made me change my projection was getting closer to applying to dental school.

The university I was looking at only took a very select amount of students into their dental program and only four into their orthodontics program. I thought there was no way I would get in and quit. Guys, I graduated from a prestigious university with HONORS. I would have gotten in. Or at least would have had a chance! I took myself out of the running before anyone else could.

Don't do this. If you don't believe in yourself, borrow some of my belief in you. I'm telling you, you CAN do it. Do you want to go back to school to be a nurse? GO FREAKING DO IT! Want to build your own business, freaking go! Whatever it is. If you have desire and a work ethic you can do it. You are the only one who can say it's over. There's always another way to try. So, please! Don't worry. Have some freaking belief in yourself to at least TRY what you want to do. Don't take yourself out of the game before it even starts.

HOW AM I GOING TO GET THERE?

Once you have a clear idea of what you would like to chase, you then start asking yourself how do I get there? What path do I need to take? Especially in our world today, there are a million different ways to get to your goal. I have four college degrees....Clearly, I was raised to believe that education was the key to everything. While I don't regret any of my education I'm not sure college is always the answer. It's AN answer. You should definitely look at college and see what it can do for you. For many people, a college degree still goes a LONG way. And if you want to be a teacher or a doctor clearly you must go to college. But for many goals, trade schools are awesome. For others, all you need is the internet and ambition to get to where you want. I encourage you to look at ALL options. Do not leave any option unobserved.

For example, if this was me right now and I knew I wanted to be a writer, I would get out one of my journals and write "Writer" really big in the middle of the page. I'd then use my beloved Google to search out as many ways as I could possibly find on how to get to that goal. College writing degree, writing for contests, freelance writing, copy editing, advertising writer....the list can go on and on. I would write out every single option and then begin the process of figuring out which option was for me.

A big one here is not to be afraid of unconventional methods. Everyone thought making vlogs on YouTube was insane until the first few got super successful and rich. Now people try every single day to construct what others have done before them. While I will always say to make sure your bills are paid and your family is taken care of, when it comes to achieving your goals, do not be afraid of new and unconventional methods. The jobs some of you are going to hold in the future haven't even been developed yet. So don't be afraid to be an early adopter. Try something. You never know if it's going to work.

As far as deciding which route to go- college, trade school, or going straight to a career- no one can really answer this but you. You have to put in the time to look through the information and decide what's best for you. Again, the people and support system of the place you go, is what's really important. If you want a strong Christian community, don't attend a college for devil worshipers. It's that simple but also can be that hard. I always tell people to look for an environment where they will continue to grow and become who they are meant to be. Most degrees or certificates are all equal. Unless you are going to Harvard or something crazy, an accredited degree is an accredited degree. But it's the experiences and opportunities you receive while earning the degree that will set you apart. Real-life experiences are what you need. Find a place that allows and supports your growth. This is why there are so many options. Every one of us needs something different. Find your place and don't be afraid to go all in.

IS IT GOOD ENOUGH?

One of my favorite memories growing up in small-town Kansas was eating Hamburger Helper (off-brand, of course) and watching the hilarious sitcom Home Improvement. If you haven't seen it, or Lord forbid you are too young to even know what it is, it is a show of an everyday family of five just trying to do life. Within these perimeters are all the funny everyday problems a husband, father, or even kids run into. One of the most popular episodes debuts "The Look". Whenever one of the men on the show says or does something dumb the wife rears up and gives him the most snarky and glaring look from across the room. The reactions from the other cast members bring laugh tracks straight from the 90's.

The "Look" is what I get every single day from students obsessing over their futures. I sometimes call it the glaze. It's that glazed-over, paralyzed stare into the abyss that is driven by fear. This look has penetrated my soul and broken it over and over again. This look hurts me. This look makes me want to reach out to each student and scream advice and care into them. I know the pain and emptiness that accompanies this "look". It's as if the beholder is looking for someone, anyone really, to just tell them what to do.

The "look" I will NEVER forget came from a girl named Emily. I found Emily hidden away in the corner of the commons area with a full set of tears spilling down her face. To give you some background information, Emily was a very smart and likable girl. She had friends, was involved in a few key things at school, and earned top grades. She had an idea of what she wanted to do in college and as a career. She believed she could do anything within reason and really wanted to do something great with her life. This is a student many from the outside would think had it all. Senior year had come around, and she had begun to apply at schools and for scholarships. To her expectations, offers for admission and some scholarships began to roll in. She began sorting through her options and trying to decide on where to go. Along came a great scholarship worth $40,000 to a wonderful small state school that had her program offering. As her teacher, my excitement screamed across my entire being. Until I noticed "The Look"...

"What's the problem?" I asked her.

"It's local." Emily responded.

"So what? It's an amazing school!" I lashed out trying to catch myself. "What's wrong?"

"I don't know. I just can't commit."

"It doesn't have a wow factor does it?"

"No!!! That's it! That's exactly it!"

Emily had no idea what was keeping her from being as excited as I was. Basically, a free ride to an amazing school with her program should make ANYONE excited, but she just couldn't be! What was wrong with it? She thought. What was wrong with her? We went on to have a conversation lasting an entire block period about the Wow Factor. She wanted something bigger (in her mind). She wanted something huge and Instagram-worthy. She had dreams of taking a first-day picture of her walking into the collegiate front gates in her first-day outfit (a way to pick out freshmen) that she would post with the most perfect and well-thought-out quote or lyric. She was ready to show the world, well the social media world, what she was made of. And a local college, no matter how amazing, was just not the Wow she was looking for.

I, myself, have fallen victim to the Wow Factor more than once! I was much like Emily, but sports played a major role. I knew from an early age I wanted to play ball in college and had my eye on the prize. Come high school, I had softball offers at multiple schools as well as dance scholarships. In my mind, I had a level of Wow Factor I NEEDED to accomplish. No private school or community college offering was going to do it for me. I wanted everyone to see and acknowledge how hard I had worked. (Trust me, I know how this sounds, I'm just being honest here). I had a D1 offering, some D11, a ton of community college and private school offerings, and then throw a boy into the mix and it's safe to say "the look" was a permanent fixture of my posture. The internal conflict was real.

I will forever remember the day I signed my papers to play ball at my first college. My parents were adamant about making a big deal about it. They told me over and over again how important it was for younger girls to see me being successful. I was already on my second set of papers since the first ones expired. I literally signed with tears in my eyes. I. Was. Pissed. I THOUGHT I wasn't being good enough. I thought I was settling. I couldn't shake the fact of wanting to have a Wow Factor scholarship opportunity. The truth was, the college I went to was an amazing opportunity and would open up more doors for me than I could imagine. But at that moment, I didn't think it was shiny enough.

Fast forward about 10 years and man had life happened. I was married, had a baby, and was teaching English. All three were things that were not ever planned. I had simply fallen into it. Once again, I found myself dreaming and wanting more. I knew I had all these dreams as a young child, shoot, even a teenager! I wanted to be a writer. I wanted to be a speaker. I wanted MORE! I always respected and loved people who wanted what I had but it was just not the Wow I wanted. I wanted something I couldn't wait to get up in the morning to get to work on. Trapped in my 20's, almost 30's, I found myself waking up and counting down the hours until I could go back to bed.

I have seen this Wow Factor lead to more anxiety about future decisions than anything else. I've seen this across all social economic statuses, races, and ages. We ALL want to feel special. We ALL want to turn to the world and say look at me! But this Wow Factor, in reality, does not exist. It is simply a figment of our imagination. This Wow Factor we are all after and feel like we must obtain isn't a picture on Instagram. It's not the college you go to, the team you play for, or the person you kiss at midnight as the ball drops on New Year's Eve. It's not the perfect Pinterest cupcakes you make for the school party, the number of miles you run on Saturday morning, or the number of bedrooms you have in your house. The Wow Factor is…

YOU.

Plain and simple. YOU. You are the Wow Factor! Who you are, who you are becoming, what you are going to accomplish or grow into in the next year, all of that is the Wow Factor! Everything you have already done or have been is the Wow Factor! Did you finally go for a walk after months of beating yourself up about your weight? Wow Factor. Did you decide to go to college and continue your education? Wow Factor. Are you loving your sweet babies every day the best way you can that day? Wow Factor. Are you working full-time in a job and being a consistent worker? Wow Factor! YOU are the stinking Wow Factor!!!! You are OOZING Wow Factor from every pore of your body! I NEED you to believe that, because I wouldn't lie to you. I have no reason to lie to you. More than that, I already care enough about you NOT to lie. So you can trust me when I say YOU ARE THE WOW FACTOR. So stop seeking something that isn't there. Go seek after your amazing self!

CONCLUSION:

The last thing I want to say when thinking about your future is to have goals but enjoy where you are at as well. I have so many goals. Like, crazy amounts of goals. This past year, in January, I got really serious and mentally pumped up. I was going to make things happen! I was going to publish my book, finish losing weight, redo my entire house...the list was endless. While mindset is so important, after a couple of weeks into the new year I got REALLY depressed. More than the normal teacher January depression. I lost all joy. I wasn't happy doing anything in my daily life.

I figured out what I did was in order to pump myself up to stay focused, I mentally made myself unsatisfied with everything in my current world. I guess you could say I overshot it. I love my current life. There are so many great things going on. I began writing down the great things in my life every morning. It reset my mind to think about the amazing things going on every day while still being focused on where I want to go.

This is such important advice. Have goals. Dream freaking HUGE! But admire all of the great things going on in your life TODAY. I can't imagine spending my entire life focused on the future just to not have a future. Or, be so focused on what's next that you forget to stop and enjoy the people you are with currently.

Conclusion

Yeah, so being a girl is tough. Within these pages, I have barely scratched the surface of everything you will go up against in your life. I also guarantee I've already learned hundreds of more lessons since writing it. But I hope something here has helped you. I hope it's at least a START in how to handle this insane life of being female. I also hope you have seen that even at my weakest moments, the times I was on the floor sobbing or broken to the point of complete numbness, I was never out of the game. It was never over. There is ALWAYS a lesson to learn along the way and a better you waiting on the other side. I don't know a lot of things in this life, but I know without a doubt you are WORTHY of great things, and you can have those things if you have faith and never give up. Be reflective, grateful, and stubborn beyond belief.

You'll make it. I promise.

    Love Your Friend,

    Turley

Acknowledgements

Bill:

None of this would have been possible without your undying belief and support. You pick up my slack when I can't go anymore and assure me I can do anything. You have been the biggest factor in the BEAUTIFUL transformation, that is my life. I will never have the words to express just how thankful I am for you and how much I love you.

No matter how much time I have with you, it will never be enough. You are my favorite person to do crazy things with as well as simply sitting on the couch with the dog. I can't wait to see what's to come!!!

Matt:

I would NOT be here today without you. I will never be able to thank you enough for believing in me when I didn't believe in myself. I'm okay with letting myself down, but once you wanted to be a part of the project, I refused to let you down. The amount of time and work you have put into this book is incalculable. I truly hope someday I can write you the check you deserve.

As sad as I am to think about you graduating next year, I KNOW you are going to go on and do REMARKABLE things. I am so proud of everything you are and can't wait to see all that you do!

Joely:

I'm so glad you decided to grab a camera a few years ago and follow a passion to capture moments to remember. I'm even more glad you stumbled into Emerge where I got to teach you for the first time. You will ALWAYS be one of my "kids".

You are wise beyond your years and I KNOW you are going to do amazing things. Whether you decide to stay taking photos, become a teacher, or something completely different, I can't wait to be cheering you on the entire time!

Chloe:

Every single day you pop into my classroom you make my day a MILLION times better! Your creativity and the ideas you brought to this project were game-changing!!! I'm not sure where we would have been without you on our team!

I am SO thankful to have gotten the chance to be your teacher. You have a joy and light that the world is desperate for. I will be uber sad when you graduate, but I CANNOT wait to see you spread that joy everywhere you go!

My Lunch Group:

Thank you for eating your variety of lunches in my cluttered, crazy room every single day. You guys bring so much joy to my days! You all have been the BIGGEST supporters and best HYPE team!!!!

Every single one of you is going to do incredible things. You will all go in very different directions but if you stay true to the awesomeness you are, I KNOW you are going to do life-changing things!

Charleigh:

No one understands how hard it's been to both support your momma and also want more of her at the same time. I have struggled your entire life to find a balance between being everything for you and also modeling what it means to go after your dreams. I pray daily that what I've done has helped and inspired you more than anything else.

Thank you for changing my life forever. I LOVE watching you be authentically you every, single, day! I hope and pray you keep that crazy awesome confidence that beams from the most beautiful smile on this planet. I love you more than you will ever know!

Beatrice:

I am so thankful you were added to my life! I know it hasn't always been easy sharing your father with me but I hope you know I will never take that sweet man for granted.

You are becoming the most INCREDIBLE person! Every day you do and try things that blow me away. I am SO proud of everything you are and everything you will be! Thank you for always being my biggest hypeman!!!

Mom:

Despite all the crazy decisions I made growing up, thank you for always being my rock. There aren't enough apologies left in me to say sorry for all the pain, worry, and sleepless nights I gave you. The most important thing I remember you telling me throughout my years, was that NO MATTER WHAT, I could always come home. There wasn't anything terrible enough that would prevent you from loving me. THIS is the reason I've grown into such a reflective person. I had permission to be.

I'm not sure what I did to win the mom lottery but I am THANKFUL for it! You were everything to both of us growing up. The biggest lesson you ingrained in us is to trust the Lord in everything we do. I have no idea where I'd be without that influence. You are now my best friend and EVERYTHING to my daughter. We will NEVER be able to show you just how much we love you!!! I hope and PRAY I can be half the mom you are for us!

Dad:

Thank you for digging into the awful things I'll never understand to heal yourself. I am BEYOND thankful for the weird, odd, amazing relationship we have today. I thank the Lord every day for recovery and strength!

My favorite thing to watch you do is be a Papa. You are the most loving and greatest grandpa Charleigh and Paxton could ever have. I will always remember our first outing where we walked around Legends people-watching. I knew in that moment our future was going to be great. I can't wait to make a million more memories with you!

Chuck:

First of all, I'm sorry for all the crap and annoyance you had to put up with from me. I KNOW being my older brother wasn't always fun or easy. But I am SO thankful for all the time, advice, and love you put into my life. I hope you know just how special you are to me.

To watch and emulate you growing up has been a privilege. I couldn't have had anyone better forging the way for me. I am SO proud of everything you have become and are continuing to be. Thank you for being the best brother I could ever ask for!

Grandma Day:

My creativity and ability to dream came from the wonderful days I spent watching you explore and dream. I can't imagine where I'd be today without you being there dreaming up fake cities and fun treasure hunts. My imagination is what it is, because of the time YOU invested in it!

Thank you for kicking down barriers for ladies like me. I'm sure you were an anomaly at the time but I am SO grateful to have been raised by such STRONG women! This is all because of the example you set forth. I treasure every single moment I've had with you. I LOVE you more than I'll ever be able to express! Thank you for being one of my biggest fans!!!

GRANDMA TRISH:

Thank you so much for joining our family and loving me like your own. I have SUCH cherished memories of spending long weekends with you and Grandpa. The love I feel walking through your front door is immeasurable!

Thank you for showing me what it means to be a God-fearing woman! Thank you for showing me it's okay to be myself in this world. I love you so very much!!!

TRAVIS:

For seven long years, you believed and prayed for this book. Regardless, of where we are now, I KNOW those prayers did not go unanswered. I thank you for every single one of them.

Finally, thank you LORD for never giving up on me! Thank you for my calling to be a writer and helping me get there. I'm so grateful your grace never runs out. Everything I write, speak, or do, is in honor of You.

Made in the USA
Middletown, DE
06 September 2024